THE MYSTERY OF
CHRISTIAN WORSHIP

ODO CASEL

THE MYSTERY OF
CHRISTIAN WORSHIP

Edited by

Burkhard Neunheuser, O.S.B.

Introduction by

Aidan Kavanagh, O.S.B.

A Herder & Herder Book

The Crossroad Publishing Company

New York

The Crossroad Publishing Company
370 Lexington Avenue, New York, NY 10017

Original edition: *Das Christliche Kultmysterium*, © 1932 by Verlag Friedrich Pustet, Regensburg. This is a translation of the fourth edition, published by Verlag Friedrich Pustet in 1960.
Chapters 2-5 are revised and enlarged versions of articles originally published as follows:
Chapter 2 in *Liturgische Zeitschrift* 3 (1930/31) 39-53; 72-83; 105-115.
Chapter 3 in *Bayerische Blätter für das Gymnasialschulwesen* 63 (1927) 329-40.
Chapter 4 in *Liturgische Zeitschrift* 4 (1931/32) 37-44.
Chapter 5 in the first edition of *Die Betende Kirche* (1924) 182-206, published by Maria Laach.

English translation © 1962 by Darton, Longman and Todd, London

Nihil obstat: Joannes M. T. Barton, S.T.D., L.S.S., Censor deputatus

Imprimatur: Georgius L. Craven, Vic.Gen., Epus. Sebastopolis, Westmonasterii, die 30a Aug. 1960.

Printed in the United States of America

Library of Congress Cataloging-in-Publication Data
Casel, Odo, 1886-1948.
    [Christliche Kultmysterium. English]
    The mystery of Christian worship / Odo Casel ; edited by
Burkhard Neunheuser ; introduction by Aidan Kavanagh.
        p.   cm. — (Milestones in Catholic theology)
    Includes bibliographical references and index.
    ISBN 0-8245-1808-X (pbk.)
    1. Catholic Church—Liturgy.   2. Paschal mystery.
I. Neunheuser, Burkhard, 1903-   . II. Title. III. Series.
BX1970.C3213   1999
264'.02—dc21   99-11630
                                                    CIP

1 2 3 4 5 6 7 8 9 10   03 02 01 00 99

CONTENTS

LIST OF ABBREVIATIONS

A.L.W.   Archiv für Liturgiewissenschaft
J.L.W.   Jahrbuch für Liturgiewissenschaft

INTRODUCTION

Odo Casel (1886-1948) was a monk of the Abbey of Maria Laach in Germany, near Bonn. A deeply spiritual and learned man, he lived through what might be called the worst years of the twentieth century, especially for Germany, in which millions died in two catastrophic world wars that left his country all but ruined along with much of the rest of Europe. Yet reading him one would hardly know such things took place, the mark of a true contemplative. He died in the aftermath of World War II while celebrating the Easter Vigil, it is said, just after he had finished singing the *Lumen Christi* as he bore the great Easter candle into the darkened church—a blessed death indeed.

Casel first published *Das christliche Kultmysterium,* of which this book is a translation, in 1932. It was controversial from the beginning, not reaching wide acceptance until over thirty years later with the publication of the Constitution on the Sacred Liturgy of the Second Vatican Council (December 4, 1963). The break with the conventional view of the liturgy begun by Casel and made formal by the Council was profound, and it is in this break (not always known or appreciated today) that Casel's import can best be seen.

THE CHURCH IN THE
EARLY TWENTIETH CENTURY

The Church into which Casel was born was different in many ways from that of today. For ordinary people the Sunday Mass was their usual contact with the Church, regarded by many as made up of the clergy and religious supported by the laity, who followed a passive role in most religious matters, including the liturgy. As is often the case, the actual form the liturgy took signaled the way the Church itself was regarded. In this instance, a passive laity at Mass reflected a view of the Church as a temporal state made of active "aristocracies" over passive, even disenfranchised, lower classes, the whole governed by laws interpreted by lawyers. There was little room for mystery and beauty was disregarded. The clergy possessed the official liturgy approved by lawful authority; the laity attended without much if any participation, occupying themselves in reciting the Rosary or with other devotions that the lawyers made clear were *not* liturgy because they were not contained in the officially approved books issued by Rome with papal assent.

Having no "essential" part in the clergy's official liturgy, the laity over many generations had created their own vernacular forms of worship that occupied them during the usually silent Mass of the priest. There were few if any communions, but the Sunday Mass often ended with both clergy and people together venerating the Real Presence of Christ in the Host by Benediction of the Blessed Sacrament.

This sort of polity was neither accidental nor arbitrary. It had evolved over the centuries since the Conciliar Movement (thirteenth through fifteenth centuries) and the Reformation (sixteenth century) had spawned traumas for the western Church. To make matters even worse, new ones had arisen: Enlightenment rationalism, revolutions in America and France, the rise of scientific method that often challenged faith, Romanticism and persecution throughout Europe, the *Risorgimento* in Italy that reduced the temporal power of the popes (nineteenth century)—all this had produced a highly disciplined but defensive church.

While all these were general influences, about which much more could and, perhaps, should be said, there was one that was a function of them all: the condemnation of "modernism" by Pius X in 1907, an event seen by many as in continuity with Pius IX's Syllabus of Errors (1864). With some justification, both of these condemnations highlighted modern excesses, but they were used by some as censures applying to all intellectual endeavors that led into any territory that was not entirely familiar, even including those that drew inspiration from the array of newly restored disciplines such as scriptural, liturgical, and patristic studies. Given the depth of Casel's involvement in such studies, whose aim was a more profound grounding in the Tradition of the Church in its entire range, to accuse him of "modernism" was absurd, though some did exactly that. I recall a seminary lecture on "modernism" in the late 1950s that attacked the scholarly work of the great German historian Adolf von Harnack (1851-1930) as being "modernist." According to the lecturer, Harnack's "modernism" was conclusively demonstrated by the fact that he had once been a monk of Maria Laach. Actually, of course, Harnack—a life-long Protestant—was never a monk at Maria Laach or anywhere else. The lecturer had, breathtakingly, dismissed Harnack, Casel (indirectly, however, since Casel was being read at the time), Maria Laach, and scholarly studies as being somehow unCatholic according to his own view of Pius IX's and Pius X's condemnations of "modernism."

A RETURN TO ANCIENT SOURCES

All these influences bore on Casel, especially after 1907 when "modernism" became an important issue in many quarters of the Church. From his historical and patristic studies, and from his own experience, Casel became aware that when the Fathers of the Church spoke of the liturgy and the Church they did not always mean the same thing that modern Catholics did. Between Casel and the Fathers much water had roared under the bridge: the Reformation and Counter Reformation, Scholasticism and neo-scholasticism, and the Industrial Revolution that deracinated many in the eighteenth and nineteenth centuries with consequent loosening of people's bonds to the Church. Social volatility and revolutions against old-style governments grew from the mid-nineteenth century and bedeviled Europe throughout Casel's lifetime, culminating in Russian Bolshevism and Western Fascism.

Of all this many Church apologists seem to have been unaware. A certain absence in them of any degree of well-informed historical consciousness was, ironically, responsible for the "modernism" panic as well as for the tilt toward mere ideology among many theologians and, especially, among European politicians. Suppress or be ignorant of history and one can absolutize any unfounded notion or yearning one's heart may desire. Casel would certainly have had ample opportunity to examine this in the Germany of the 1920s and 30s had he cared to look.

This is not to say that his motivation was politics, whether civil or ecclesiastical. The Rule of Benedict, under which Casel lived, urged him to the books of the Bible and the writings of the Apostolic Fathers, and it is here that Casel found insight worth recovering, not in the coils of political ideology and current events. Thus the roots of his teaching lay in the deep rich soil of Scripture, the Fathers, and the Graeco-Roman cultural milieu of patristic thought and liturgy.

CASEL'S MYSTERY THEOLOGY

Tutored by these magnificent teachers, Casel came at what was needful on a plane that far surpassed politics and mere ideology. He also rather sidestepped internal Church debates, never succumbing to the temptations of controversy despite those that swirled around at least some of his work. Given the state of Church and theology at the time, Casel offered revolutionary theses that ran counter to received notions of Church and sacrament, but the growing crises in Europe largely overshadowed the publicity his work might otherwise have received until after the Second World War. The encyclicals of Pius XII, *Mystici Corporis* (1945) and *Mediator Dei* (1947), reveal some influence by Casel's mystery theology—at least Casel thought so—as does the Constitution on the Sacred Liturgy of the Second Vatican Council (1963).

What Casel taught was really quite simple but revolutionary for its time. He said that more was (and had to be) present in a sacrament than graces for the faithful, or even the Body and Blood of Christ in the Eucharist. Although graces and the Real Presence were certainly involved, something prior to them and enabling of them was crucial: the active presence of the saving mystery of the incarnate Christ—not just graces nor even the Body and Blood of Christ otherwise really absent and in heaven. This was to tread on many pious toes, not all of which belonged just to the laity.

Casel went farther out on the limb, however, when he appealed to Romans ch.6, the very text Martin Luther used in his theology of justification by faith alone. But Casel found it crucial in his mystery theology to emphasize our participation in the passion and death of Christ: we do not, obviously, die the *same* death

Christ died, nor do we rise in the *same* manner that he did. Paul says that in baptism we die a death *like (homoioma)* his and are granted a resurrection *like (homoioma)* his. The key word, *homoioma*, means far more than "like" or "similar to": it means "conformed to." Thus Christ died once and for all on a cross and rose once and for all from a tomb in Jerusalem: our death and rising in baptism are conformed to his so closely that we may say that we have died and risen *in* his death, <u>in</u> his resurrection. He died and rose once only and by grace allows us, not to die as he did, but by our baptismal conformation to him to die our own death in him and to rise in him. Our lives have become one with his, and his with ours. The doctrines of grace and the Real Presence as well as all of Christian spirituality flow from here. To be "justified" is to be conformed to Christ, by Christ, and in Christ by grace, faith, and sacramental participation in His saving mystery. Those who do this are called the Church, Christ's Body—a great and holy mystery if ever there was one.

The core of Casel's teaching is that in the liturgy, as in the Church more generally, Christ is present not just as the object of our pious memory but present in his saving acts — he dies not again but *still*, rises not again but *still*—in us, by us, and through us for the life of the world. Christ does not pass out graces to those who follow him if they behave themselves. He gathers them lovingly into himself as he conquers from the Cross and rises from the grave, in the liturgy as in the Church. This is the Mystery the liturgy celebrates, the Mystery the Church cherishes as its source and center. In the true celebration of the Mystery there is nothing that is anthropocentric, rationalistic, subjective, or sentimental; rather, it finds expression in a rigorous theocentrism, objective contemplation, and a splendid transcendentalism. The Mystery is, after all, divine at its source.

CASEL'S INFLUENCE

The more I have contemplated Casel's vision over the past forty years, the more I have come to see its brilliance and simplicity. The book is not a technical treatise but a piece of popular spiritual writing. This may, oddly, be its Achilles' Heel: the term "Mys-

tery" has been so assimilated into the mindset and patois of ecclesiastical writers since the Second Vatican Council—which em-
braced Casel's teaching—that it has become slick with use and
thus barely one-dimensional. One writer on the Sacred Mysteries
cites Casel only once, in a footnote, because he introduced the
term "mystery" again in the West—almost damnation with faint
praise.

Really to assay Casel's stature one must read him against the
historical background of his time. Many Enlightenment intellectu-
als gave wary approval to religion as a comfort to some people and
as an agent of good social order even as they deplored its irrational, mythological, and superstitious core. The temptation they
offered religion, Christianity in particular, was state protection so
long as it helped the state control the masses. This notion produced a desiccated religion asleep on the breast of rationalism—
Lenin's opiate of the people. But late-nineteenth-century scholar-
ship, in rediscovering the great religious traditions of Egypt and
the East, found spirituality, miracles, mysticism, and mystery
serving the birth and development of cultures as the most critical
forces of social cohesion.

Odo Casel was a child of this rediscovery, which through him
and others emerged powerfully in the Second Vatican Council, especially in its Constitution on the Sacred Liturgy: "Nevertheless
the liturgy is the summit toward which the activity of the Church
is directed, it is also the fount from which all her power flows"
(para. 10). These words, written by others fifteen years after his
death, are the very essence of his book, first published almost
thirty years earlier.

The gradual spread of the core of Casel's teaching on the mystery of Christian worship has reinvigorated not just talk about the
liturgy but also about sacraments and the Church, the former seen
as acts of worship, the latter as the redeemed community at worship, and the Mystery of God in Christ as the source and summit
of it all.

Aidan Kavanagh, O.S.B.
Yale University

I

THE MYSTERY AND MODERN MAN

'THOU sparest all things, Lord, lover of souls, for they are thine: in all is thine imperishable Spirit. Therefore it is that thou dost chastise but tenderly those who wander from the way, and make them mindful of their sins, reproaching them, that, freed from evil, they may have faith in thee.'[1]

God indeed allows men freely to go their way, for he has made them free. But his living breath, his holy spirit, his action, are in all: man is never wholly alone. This is the ground for that astonishing fact of history, that mankind is always being re-*generated*, that is re-acquiring a new spirit. We can observe this renewal today when changes in human life are occurring as perhaps never before; certainly at no time have men stood so in need of a 'turning', of *conversio* in the original meaning of the word, of the new life, as in our day. For never have they wandered so far away from the Mystery of God, or stood so near to death.

'The fool hath said in his heart "there is no God".'[2] This foolishness has reached its height in the millions who call themselves 'godless', and who, by the very use of this purely negative word, show the emptiness and insecurity of their revolt.

The Mystery of God, who dwells above all creatures in limitless majesty, whose action influences the most insignificant human event, whose wisdom is all surpassing and boundless, whose power cannot be overcome; this God of mystery has become a burden to man, a burden of which he would gladly be quit, in order to go his own way unhindered. He will have no eternal law or independent will above himself; he wants to be free of every tie not of his own making, to be his own last end, his own ruler, servant to no-one, subject to no-one. Nature is his to master, it is to become his empire and the subject of his scientific, merely rational, investigations. There is no world of the irrational, no 'other'. There is only matter, which is to be subjected to factual investigations.

So it has come about that nature, too, has lost her mystery. The cosmos is emptied of its spiritual content, or rather emptied of it in such a

[1]Wisdom 11, 26–12, 2.   [2]Ps. 13, 1; 52, 1.

measure as never before; nature is no longer symbol, a transparency of higher realities. She breathes no secrets which make man cry: 'Such wisdom as thine is far beyond my reach, no thought of mine can attain it'.[1] Man has explored the deepest reaches of nature; every day the earth loses size and depth. Now, just as he has broken into the smallest atom, he is prepared to step off into space and win for himself the secrets of the stars. Nature, dethroned and stripped bare, has nothing left to it except the business of making man's life easier and more pleasant; vast sums of money are amassed and spent in order to make every material thing quickly available to all; applied science works its miracles, and lays the earth at the feet of man for him to use and to control. That strange curse which God pronounced after the Fall, that men should make their daily work a mystery of reparation and give it meaning for another life seems to have been extinguished. Poverty, sickness and pain, which were also to remind man of that other realm, have been fought with undreamed-of success; death itself is put off as long as possible; the life-span is almost double that earlier generations expected. The mystery of death is so far as possible kept covered and out of public sight; there are those who dream of doing away with it altogether, or proclaim its end as an ideal for the 'golden future'.

Still, though the outer world had been deprived of its secrets, there might have remained the unsearchable depths of the human soul. But these depths, too, have been probed and subjected to the searchlight of psycho-analysis; what glimmers there has been revealed as a confused mass of half-suppressed, sensual desires and wishes, more inspiring repulsion and fear than any other reaction. Love, religion, friendship, ideals—all have been exploded as mere nervous twitchings. With this, reverence for the mystery of the other person, or for the community disappears. How can any man exercise public functions as an instrument of divine authority, how can he hope for love and respect from those in his charge? How can the community demand the service of the individual, to include, on occasion, the sacrifice of his life? Society cannot stand for anything greater than the individual himself. No, man is an atom among other atoms; let him enjoy his span of life, and that to the fullest extent possible. There is no 'love' which can, by the gift of itself to another person or to the community, raise the individual into a new dimension of existence. It is usual nowadays to talk a great deal about the brotherhood of nations and service to humanity; but behind all this

[1]Ps. 138, 6.

there is not that deeper love which is a sharing in the very love of God himself, his *agape*, but instead the self-divinization of mankind, which sees in itself the god it means to worship. Community means nothing except individuals lumped in a mass, joined together for the sole purpose of fighting off, by their collective weight, any power which might make a claim to rule over them: a spectacle of brute power.

Modern man thinks that he has thus finally driven out the darkness of the Mystery, and that he stands at last in the clear light of sober reason and self-conscious, autonomous will, for the first time truly master of the world. But what happened at the dawn of history has repeated itself. Then, too, at the moment when man believed that he had obtained godhead by his own power, that he could recognize by the light of his own understanding what was good and evil, that he had come of age and needed no parental care, in that moment he 'saw that he was naked'.[1] He recognized his shame, saw himself as a king in disgrace, a monarch without a throne. The sin of our first parents becomes not merely an infectious poison in successive generations; it is repeated over and over again in each. And every time the result is the same: the revolutionary becomes a slave. Today this slavery is perhaps at its worst, when the revolutionary imagines he has freed himself from all bonds whatever. He is in fact not subject to individual human tyrants, but rather to much worse and more cruel impersonal powers, whose rule he can never shake off. The last road to freedom, which in antiquity was open even to the slave, modern man has closed up to himself: the road to God. He remains wholly circumscribed in the bounds of the material world. By imagining he is the ruler of this world, he is forced more and more to do its will; soulless machine and dead money master him, and demand blood offerings, the sale of his heart and mind: a pitiful end to the great age of individualism which had seemed to have begun with so much attraction and promise for the future.

For, if the last results of an age of individualism inspire us with something less than admiration, we must not forget how deceptively attractive those beginnings were. The men of the early Renaissance seem to wander through a lovely countryside in the full bloom of springtide; the age of Gothic was proudly conscious that it had climbed out of the shadows, away from the weary ponderousness of the Romanesque, out of the secret atmosphere of the crypts, and into the clear light of day, and of a reasonable, bright human culture.

[1]Gen. 3, 7.

No mystery hovered over that era captivating the minds of men, hiding the nature of reality. Reason, *ratio*, made itself felt in every sphere of life, stripping creation of its quality of wonder to the curious eyes of man, with the result that there seemed to be ever less and less place in the universe for the action of God. Since that time 'science' has had the effect of more and more breaking the bonds of faith, and has run on from triumph to triumph. For its part, the emancipated will has strained itself to even greater titanic efforts, and, in Promethean pride, worked marvels of invention.

Nor did the new spirit leave the sphere of religion and the church untouched.* The West, of course, did on the whole remain faithful to the old religion. But the attempt was made, nonetheless, to exhaust the secrets of God's revelation with reason; to dissect it, and to 'demonstrate' its truth. Mathematical thought, the most typical product of man's abstractive faculty, was set to work among the humanities, and even in theology. Natural science, disinterested in the action of a higher being, was discovering laws of evolution in all living beings, and sought to apply this principle to the dogmas of the church, as well as other things.

Then, too, emphasis on the autonomy of will showed itself in a departure from the traditional theology which had made God the Alpha and Omega of being, his will all-active, and human will and perfection his gift. In the piety of this period, next to God stands man, free, independent, seeking his own way to God, no longer raised up by God to himself. The lone individual fights in solitary battle for the heights; the church as the mother of graces moves into the background. Thus a new conception arose in the life of piety with a carefully adjusted psychology adapting itself to each individual, and methods of interior life calculated to stimulate each individual's gifts.

The clear consequence of this was a withdrawal of emphasis on the church's mystery. It put too much emphasis on the secret activity of God's grace, on the involvement and co-operation in action between God and man, in which man was the receiving partner, too much emphasis on the *ecclesia* as mother, bringing the individual into the common life. It was too little open to the view of 'reason' and to proof; its content was too difficult to grasp and yielded too few measurable results; laid too great a task upon the purpose of 'personality' and the 'greatest happiness

*The asterisks which occur in the text or the notes refer the reader to the Editor's notes on pp. 94–97.

of men', being all for God and the holy fellowship. In short, it was too simple, too uncomplicated, too much God's affair to suffice for the man who had come to such consciousness of his own powers. Rationalism and mystery do not go well together.

Our time has brought the fall of rationalism and a new turning to the mystery. The humanization of religion had progressed so far that, finally, there was no religion left. For this reason many doubted religion, which no longer held them with any inward grasp, did not bind them, was no longer something greater than they. Others, with more justification, have returned to a richer belief. They are seeking once more the ancient image of God in majesty and boundless greatness, the God who leaves human things far behind him, and 'raises man up when he crushes him'. The God of power, whom the prophets showed, and the unfathomable *agape* which made itself known on the cross, to mankind's amazement reveal anew the glory of this Godhead. Man comes once more to see that God is all in all, that his power fills all things, his will rules over them, his love penetrates them. He realizes that he himself first acquires greatness when he becomes nothing before this mystery. He senses once more the deep harmony between God and creation; the world becomes for him once more a stage on which God's drama is being carried out, a symbol of thoughts which reach beyond it. God's mystery once again inspires dread, attracts and calls us.

The mystery means three things and one. First of all it is God considered in himself, as the infinitely distant, holy, unapproachable, to whom no man may draw near and live; in likeness to whom everything is impure, as the prophet said: 'I am a man of unclean lips, dwelling in the midst of a people with unclean lips; and I saw the Lord, the King of battles, with my own eyes.'[1] And this all-holy one reveals his mystery, comes down to his creatures and reveals himself to them; yet once again, *in mysterio*, that is to say, in a revelation by grace, to those whom he has chosen, the humble, the pure of heart, not to the proud and the self-important. Hence his revelation remains a mystery, because it is not open to the profane world, but hides itself, shows itself only to the believers, the ones whom he has chosen.

God's being, then, is infinitely above the world; yet by grace he dwells within his creatures, within mankind: he is at once transcendent and immanent. In essence he surpasses all he has made, yet penetrates it everywhere, by his presence and his action.

[1]Isaiah 6, 5.

The ancient world had a shadowy foreboding of the mystery. It knew that all the things of earth are only the reflection and creation of a glory that surpasses them. This foreboding of the mystery brought forth the temples of the Sumerians and Babylonians and the pyramids and sphinx of the Egyptians with their air of eternity. In Greece the deep things of platonic wisdom speak of it; the mystery-cults in the Classical and Hellenistic age approach it. Everywhere there is longing to bring heaven down into the world, to bring man nearer to God, and marry the two hemispheres.

In the case of the Jews, God himself gave approval to this longing by his revelation. It is true that the Law strongly sharpened the boundaries between God and man. It was the barrier around the holy mountain where God ruled. But the prophets went on speaking in new and ever more detailed pictures of God's approaching kingdom, of the time when he would pitch his tent among his own people and his Spirit would penetrate all flesh.

God's coming in the flesh fulfilled and more than fulfilled all longing and all promise; this event gave the word *mysterium* a new and deepened meaning. For St Paul μυστήριον is the marvellous revelation of God in Christ. God, the one who hides in everlasting silence, 'who dwells in inapproachable light, whom no man has seen nor can'[1] has revealed himself in the flesh; the *Logos*, his Son, has become man, and in a way which escapes our grasping, has shown the wholeness of his Father's love on the Cross. 'God gave proof of his love for us: it was while we were still sinners that he died for us.'[2] John says the same thing in other words: 'No man has seen God; the only-begotten Son who is in the Father's bosom, he has declared it to us.'[3] In the Son of God made man and crucified we look upon the mystery of God which was hidden before the ages, but through Christ is made known and revealed to the ecclesia, the body of those whom he has called.

Christ is the mystery in person, because he shows the invisible godhead in the flesh. The deeds of his lowliness, above all his sacrificial death on the cross, are mysteries because God shows himself through them in a fashion which surpasses any human measurement. Above all else, his resurrection and exaltation are mysteries because God's glory is shown through them in the human person of Jesus, although in a

[1] I Tim. 6, 16.
[2] Rom. 5, 8.
[3] Jn. 1, 18.

manner hidden to the world and open only to the knowledge of the faithful. This mystery of Christ is what the apostles proclaimed to the Church, and what the Church passes on to all generations. Yet just as the saving design is not merely teaching, but first and foremost Christ's saving deed, so, too, the church leads mankind to salvation not merely by word only, but by sacred actions; through faith and the mysteries Christ lives in the church.

Thus the mysterium acquires a third sense, which, however, is most intimately connected with the first two; since Christ is no longer visible among us, in St Leo the Great's words, 'What was visible in the Lord has passed over into the mysteries.'[1] We meet his person, his saving deeds, the workings of his grace in the mysteries of his worship. St Ambrose writes: 'I find you in your mysteries.'[2]

The meaning of the divine mystery, three-fold yet one, is the subject of this little book. The mystery is ἄρρητον, ineffable; beyond utterance, not only in the original meaning, that it might not be spoken, but further that its content cannot be exhausted by words. Everything we say of it will fall short of the mark; but just because it is ineffable, there is always occasion for saying something of it. The *pneuma* which comes from the Lord will reveal all the rest to those whose wills are ready, while the man without faith will gain no hint of its depths.

The book will speak first of the position which the mystery of worship has within the Christian scheme; then of its relationship to the mysteries of antiquity, which lend it their language; and finally of the mystery as it acts throughout the sacred year and sacred day.[3]

The turning to the mystery is a present fact; the task for each individual is to find his way to the spring of healing. For it is only the mystery of God which can heal the world again; in it the *pneuma* of God acts, the blood of Christ flows to restore the world and give it holiness, to reconcile it to God, transfigure it. Today the world outside Christianity and the church is looking for mystery; it is building a new kind of rite in which man worships himself. But through all of this the world will never reach God. Let us hold fast to the mystery of Christ, the gift the Father sent among us in the incarnate Word. To this mystery the Church with the Spirit's breath upon her has given visible countenance by the work of many hundreds of years, has made a form which,

---

[1]Sermo 74, 2, P.L. 54, 398A.
[2]*Apologia prophetae David*, 58.
[3][Casel's book on the Mass is to be published under the German title, *Das Christliche Opfermysterium*. Ed.]

unchanged in essence, yet gives the mind its freedom. We need not go looking for it, we need only give ourselves to it, go about the celebration of the bridegroom's mysteries with the church, Christ's bride; in this we shall ourselves be transformed in him, and go his way with the Son to the Father.

2

THE MYSTERY OF WORSHIP IN THE CHRISTIAN COSMOS

IF we would learn what the mystery's place is in the Christian scheme of things, we must first ask, what is the Christian scheme.

i *The Mystery of Christ*

Christianity is not a 'religion' or a confession in the way the last three hundred years would have understood the word: a system of more or less dogmatically certain truths to be accepted and confessed, and of moral commands to be observed or at least accorded recognition. Both elements belong, of course, to Christianity, intellectual structure and moral law; but neither exhausts its essence. Still less is Christianity a matter of religious sentiment, a more or less emotionally toned attitude towards 'The divine', which binds itself to no dogmatic or moral system whatever.

St Paul thinks of Christianity, the good news, as 'a mystery'; but not merely in the sense of a hidden, mysterious teaching about the things of God, a sense the word already bore in the philosophy of late antiquity.[1] Rather for him *mysterium* means first of all a deed of God's, the execution of an everlasting plan of his through an act which proceeds from his eternity, realized in time and the world, and returning once more to him its goal in eternity.[2] We can express the mystery, so

[1] Cf my book, *De philosophorum Graecorum Silentio mystico* (1919); J.L.W. 6 (1926) p. 138; 8 (1928) p. 145 ff, 225 ff; 13 (1935) p. 99 ff; 15 (1941) p. 155 ff. Also *Theologische Revue* 24 (1925) 41–47. [*Archiv für Liturgiewissenschaft* I (195c) contains a posthumous article by Dom Casel on Paul's mystery language, Ed.]*

[2] . . . 'He made known to us the mystery of his will, according to the decision which he took in him (Christ) for the design of fulfilling the ages, to sum up everything in Christ, in heaven and on the earth' (Eph. 1, 9).
'You have heard of God's saving design of grace given to me for your sakes, how revelation made known to me the mystery, as I briefly declared to you. When you read it, you will be able to see my grasp of the mystery of Christ which was not made known to the sons of men in other generations, as it has now been revealed to the holy apostles and prophets in spirit: that the nations

conceived, by the one word 'Christ'[1] meaning by it the Saviour's person together with his mystical body, the church. It embraces first of all God's incarnation, which is his last and final revelation to the world. Paul says this mystery was 'hidden' or 'unspoken before the ages', because it lay in the womb of the godhead, unknown even to the multitude of angels; hence it is called *mysterium, arcanum, secretum.* But this mystery was revealed in time, by God's taking flesh from mankind, and appearing visible to it. It is a 'revelation', an 'uncovering' in the highest and ultimate sense. Before, God spoke 'in divers ways and in divers manners, through the prophets', 'now . . . in his Son'.[2]

Yet the incarnation as such, however, does not exhaust the mystery of 'Christ'. Because of the sin of man the mystery took on the shape of economy: God's love and wisdom, planning salvation. 'The Word was made flesh, and pitched his tent among us, and we saw his glory. . . .'[3] Here John gathers together the whole saving plan. The Lord's glory was not everywhere equally recognizable and visible. Jesus became saviour, redeemer for sinners. Therefore he did not take flesh immediately in a glorified state, but rather came in 'the likeness of the sin of flesh',[4] in order to kill sin through this flesh of his. So he came in lowliness, unrecognized,[5] bearing the burden of this sin, with those of its consequences which his godhead could allow. He had no sin of his own, nor inherited any sin, for he was born of the Virgin, by the Holy Ghost. But he took up the burden of the law, bore the sorrow and the

---

are of one calling and one body and one share of the promise, in Jesus Christ, through the gospel. . . . To me the least of all the Saints this grace was given to proclaim to the heathen the unsearchable riches of Christ and to illumine all as to the design of the mystery, hidden from the ages in God the creator of all; so to the principalities and powers in heaven was to be made known through the church the manifold wisdom of God . . .' (Eph. 3, 2 ff). Cf. the parallel passages in Col. 1, 25–27 where the mystery is said to be 'Christ in you' (2, 2) and yet 'Christ' himself is 'the mystery of God.' 'We utter the hidden wisdom of God in mystery, which God predestined before the ages, for our glory' (I Cor. 2, 7). Romans 16, 25 speaks of 'the revelation of the mystery shrouded in silence for all time.' Cf. also Romans 11, 25.

[1]Col. 2, 2. For understanding the mystery of God: Christ.

[2]Heb. 1, 1 f.

[3]Jn. 1, 14.

[4]Rom. 8, 3. Cf. II Cor. 5, 21: 'He who had no knowledge of sin made himself sin so that we might become God's justice in him.'

[5]'Jesus Christ who was from the beginning by nature God, did not see in the rank of godhead a prize to be coveted; he dispossessed himself and took the nature of a slave, fashioned in the likeness of men, and presenting himself to us in human form; and then he lowered his own dignity, accepted an obedience which brought him to death, death on a cross.' (Phil. 2, 5 and 8.)

bitterness of persecution and at last the cross and death, guiltless as he was, Love brought him onto the wood, for the sins of men,[1] and when this body of his died on the cross, sin was killed with it; Satan was undone, because an innocent man has suffered pain for the guilty. Now, a new man rose, all whole and sanctified; by his obedience he had earned the right to sit beside God, and to be one with the Father forever. 'That is why God has raised him to such a height, given him that name which is greater than any other name; so that everything in heaven and on earth and under the earth must bend the knee before the name of Jesus, and every tongue must confess Jesus Christ as Lord, dwelling in the glory of God the Father.[2] The Son of man is raised to be Lord, he is no longer in the flesh of sin, but has become wholly Spirit (*pneuma*);[3] his manhood is utterly transformed by its glorification in the godhead. Everything which was merely human is past. 'Henceforward, we do not think of anybody in a merely human fashion; even if we used to think of Christ in a human fashion, we do so no longer', says St Paul.[4] This god-man, raised to be over-lord and priest, filled with glory, is the summit of God's revelation under the New Alliance.

Yet God's revelation of himself in this way is not communicated to the world at large: the world as such is not fit to see things which belong to him[5]; rather is it given to the chosen, to the saints, first of all, to 'the apostles and prophets in *pneuma*'[6] and then to all who really believe, and so to the *ecclesia*, the common body of all whom God has called.[7] To them the mystery is revealed; yet it remains a mystery because it is something which of its very nature belongs to God and is, therefore,

---

[1] I Peter 2, 22: 'he did no sin, and no lie was in his mouth: he was ill-spoken of, and spoke no evil in return, suffered and did not threaten vengeance, gave himself up to the hands of injustice. So, on the cross his body took the weight of our sins; we were to become dead to our sins and live for holiness; it was his wounds that healed.'

[2] Phil. 2, 9–11.

[3] II Cor. 3, 17: The Lord is Spirit: ὁ δὲ Κύριος τὸ πνευμά ἐστιν.

[4] II Cor. 3, 17 ff.

[5] Jn. 16, 3: 'they will do this, because they have not recognised me or the Father.' Jn. 17, 25: 'Just Father, the world has never acknowledged thee; but I have acknowledged thee, and these (the disciples) have acknowledged that thou hast sent me . . .' I Jn. 3, 1: 'the world does not know us (Christians) because it did not acknowledge the Father.' Acts 13, 27: 'the people of Jerusalem and their leaders gave to him no recognition, nor to the voices of the prophets. . . .' I Cor. 2, 8: 'No princes of the world have acknowledged it (God's wisdom in the mystery), refers to the ruling spiritual powers of this *aion*'.

[6] Eph. 3, 5.

[7] Eph., 3 10.

closed to unaided human reason, something God's grace must reveal if it is to be made known.[1]

The content of the mystery of Christ is, therefore, the person of the god-man and his saving deed for the church; the church, in turn, enters the mystery through this deed. For Paul, Peter, and John, the heart of faith is not the teachings of Christ, not the deeds of his ministry, but the acts by which he saved us.[2] 'We can see one who was made a little lower than the angels, I mean Jesus, crowned now with glory and honour for the pains of his death. . . .'[3] Through his death and resurrection, through his blood the Lord has found 'everlasting redemption'.[4] Through it he has entered the holy of holies and mounted up to God's throne; and he has made the way for us to go there also.[5] There he is high-priest[6] who gives the grace of the Spirit and creates his church.

The Christian thing, therefore, in its full and primitive meaning of

[1] I Cor. 2, 9 f: '(we proclaim): what is written, what eye hath not seen, nor ear heard, nor has it entered into man's heart, what God has prepared for those who love him. And God has revealed this through his *pneuma*.' The translation of *mysterium* by 'secret' leads to error even where it refers more to God's hidden truth, and most certainly when it clearly means God's act or the ritual action; for to the initiate to whom it is revealed, it is a secret no longer. It remains a secret to the unbeliever: to *mysterium* belongs the *revelatio* (unveiling), which still keeps the intrinsic veil of divine things. [Cf. J.L.W. 15 (1941), p. 269 ff. ed. Cf. also J. A. Robinson's note on mysterion in his Commentary on the Ephesians, Trans.]*

[2] This is particularly marked in Peter, who had been the Lord's constant companion. According to him, the *pneuma* proclaimed through the prophets, 'sufferings in Christ and the glory following upon it' (I Peter 1, 11); Christ's blood is the centre of the gospel: 'in obedience and the sprinkling with the blood of Jesus Christ' (1, 2). Christians are redeemed 'through the precious blood of Christ, the pure and spotless lamb' (1, 9). Christ is known before the creation of the world, revealed at the end of time, through Christians who believe in God through him 'who has awakened them from the dead and given them glory' (1, 20 f). The Lord's suffering is mentioned again, (2, 21 ff; 3, 18) 'with the life-breath of the Spirit', the resurrection and place at God's right hand. II Peter 1, 16 tells of Christ's transfiguration on the holy mountain, but in a form which has the whole 'epiphany' in view; the letter here stresses the second coming.

John tells in his gospel, quite naturally, of the actions of Jesus on earth; but he looks at everything in the light of the incarnate Logos' divine sonship, and selects signs which will illumine it. At the first of these we find, 'he shewed his glory and his disciples believed in him' (2, 11). At the end, 'these signs are written down, that you may believe that Jesus is the Christ, the Son of God' (20, 31). The idea of *Kyrios* in St Paul is replaced in John by the dignity of Messiah and sonship which began with the incarnation, and was made plain by the exaltation of Christ after the passion. Hence, the first epistle of St John speaks of the revelation of eternal life through the incarnation, and of the blood of Jesus which cleanses us from every sin' (1, 1). 5, 5 f sums up: 'who overcomes the world if not the one who believes that Jesus is the Son of God?' He it is who came through water and blood, Jesus Christ. In 5, 20 the *parousia* is mentioned: 'We know that the Son of God comes'.

[3] Heb. 2, 9.   [4] Heb. 9, 12.   [5] Heb. 10, 20.   [6] Heb. 9, 5 f.

God's good Word, or Christ's, is not as it were a philosophy of life with religious background music, nor a moral or theological training; it is a *mysterium* as St Paul means the word, a revelation made by God to man through acts of god-manhood, full of life and power; it is mankind's way to God made possible by this revelation and the grace of it communicating the solemn entry of the redeemed Church into the presence of the everlasting Father through sacrifice, through perfect devotion; it is the glory that blossoms out of it. At the mid-point of the Christian religion, therefore, stands the sacred *Pasch*, the passage which the Son of God who appeared in the flesh of sin, makes to the Father.[1] The pasch is a sacrifice with the consecration of the person that flows from it; it is the sacrifice of the God-man in death on the cross, and his resurrection to glory: it is the Church's sacrifice in communion with and by the power of the crucified God-man, and the wonderful joining to God, the divinization which is its effect.

Both of these sacrifices flow together; they are fundamentally one; the Church, as the woman of the new paradise and the bride of Christ, acts and offers in his strength. Christ living in time made his sacrifice alone on the cross; Christ raised up by the Spirit makes the sacrifice together with his Church which he has purified with the blood from his own side, and thus won her for himself.[2] It is not as if the Lord, now in *pneuma*, were making a new sacrifice with the Church: through the one sacrifice he has reached the term of offering, and reigns now forever at the Father's right hand; he is himself the glorified sacrificial gift. The church, not yet brought to her completion, is drawn into this sacrifice of his; as he sacrificed for her, she now takes an active part in his sacrifice, makes it her own, and is raised thereby with him from the world to God, and glorified. Thus Christ becomes the saviour of the body, and the head of the Church:[3] God has given Christ 'to the ecclesia as the head which towers over all, given him her who is his body'.[4] *

Bridegroom and bride, head and members act as one. If the man, the head is the leading actor, the stimulus to action, his bride, his members' work with him, use the power which is theirs. Christ is saviour, the one who accomplishes salvation; the church for its part

[1]Rom. 8, 3; Jo. 13, 1.
[2]Eph. 5, 25 'Husbands love your wives as Christ loved the church and gave himself up for her.'
[3]Eph. 5, 22 f.
[4]Eph. 1, 22.

shares in the act of Christ, receiving the influence of every act he does, but receiving actively; healthy members share in the action of a body. Indeed, just this makes the body a live one: a living bride, a loving bride and spouse, sharing in the actions of Christ. Every Christian is a christ, as St Augustine says,[1] 'We are to be joyful and give thanks that we are not only become Christians, but Christ'. And Methodius of Philippi in *The Banquet of the Ten Virgins*[2] says: 'The Church is with child, and lies in labour until Christ be formed in us and born in us; every one of the saints is to become Christ by participating in Christ.'

How does this participation come to be? How does a man become member of Christ? In the last analysis every participation is the work of God's grace and of eternal predestination. Upon this grace rests the first beginning of salvation's way, faith. But there is not yet the incorporation into Christ's mystical body; baptism gives this; at baptism, for the first time, the Christian meets the mystery of worship.

Christ in his human nature went through the passion and became Spirit (*pneuma*): glorified Lord (*Kyrios*), High-priest, the dispenser of the *pneuma*, and thereby head of his Church. By his sufferings he was healed[3] glorified;[4] he put aside, along with the earthly condition of his flesh, the 'sin' he had freely taken up, when he 'became sin for us' by carrying sin's weight in the manner just mentioned. This way of salvation was to be ours, too, but in Christ. He became the perfect type for us, not merely in the realm of moral action; he is the model we are to liken ourselves to in everything so far as creatures may. But we cannot do this of our own power; only through a saviour; Christ's salvation must be made real in us. This does not come about through a mere application, with our behaviour purely passive, through a 'justification' purely from 'faith', or by an application of the grace of Christ, where we have only to clear things out of the way in a negative fashion, to receive it. Rather, what is necessary is a living, active sharing in the redeeming deed of Christ; passive because the Lord makes it act upon us, active because we share in it by a deed of our own. To the action of God upon us (*opus operatum*) responds our co-operation (*opus operantis*), carried out through grace from him. How is it possible to do this great work where God and man are fellow-actors (each according to his own proper fashion; God as the master craftsman, man receiving

[1] *Tractatus in Joan.* 21, 8.
[2] Symposium 8, 8.
[3] Jn. 17, 19.
[4] Jn. 7, 39. 12, 23 (Cf 28).

what God does, yet sharing in the workmanship)? For this purpose the Lord has given us the mysteries of worship: the sacred actions which we perform, but which, at the same time, the Lord performs upon us by his priests' service in the Church. Through these actions it becomes possible for us to share most intensively and concretely in a kind of immediate contact, yet most spiritually too, in God's saving acts.

St Paul depicts for us the substance of the mystery of worship with great clearness and depth in the sixth chapter of his Epistle to the Romans* (3 ff), 'You know well enough that we who were taken up into Christ by baptism have been taken up, all of us, into his death; we have, then, been buried with him through baptism, in death, in order that as Christ rose from the dead by the Father's glory, thus we might walk in newness of life. For if we have grown up in the pattern (ὁμοιώματι) of his death, we shall share also in his resurrection. We know this, that the old man in us was crucified with him, in order to annihilate the body of sin, in order that we should no longer do slave-service to it. For the man who has died is quit of fault; if, then, we die with Christ, we believe that we shall share his life. We know that Christ, risen from the dead, dies no more; death has no more rule over him. The man who has died, has died once; the man who lives, lives for God. So you are to consider yourselves dead to sin, living for God in Christ Jesus.' To such men as these are his words directed in Colossians 3, 1–4: 'if, then, you are risen with Christ, seek the things which are above, where Christ is, sitting at God's right hand. Think of the things above, not those of earth. For you have died, and your life is hidden with Christ in God. When Christ, your life, be revealed, then you, too, will be revealed in glory.' An excellent commentary to the passage is found in Cyril of Jerusalem's second mystagogical Catechesis (5 ff*): 'O rare and paradoxical fact: we did not die as things of nature die; we were not buried in the fashion of them, nor risen after crucifixion in that way; rather it was a likening in image; but the salvation was a fact. Christ was really crucified, really buried, really rose; all this he has given us, so that we might win a real share in the likening of his sufferings. Here is surpassing love for men: Christ took the nails in his sacred hands and feet and suffered the pain; allowed me salvation through a share in its salvation without pain and without effort. Let no one, then, think that baptism is only the grace of sins' forgiveness and acceptance as a son, as John's baptism was. Rather we know that baptism was indeed the purification of sins, and the gift of the *pneuma*, but also the off-set of the sufferings of Christ; therefore St Paul has just called out to us, "you know full well" (Romans 6, 5 supra). He said this in connection with the opinion that baptism indeed gave the remission of sins and acceptance to sonship, but communion with the real sufferings of Christ by imitation of them. In order that we might all know that Christ did everything he undertook for our sakes, for the sake of our salvation, and suffered in fact not in appearance, and that we become sharers in his pain, St Paul has called out with such clarity: if we have grown up in the pattern of his death, we shall share also in his resurrection. The word "grown up" (σύμφυτοι) is meaningful; for as the true vine is emplanted here, we too are engrafted into it through sharing in the death by baptism. Give full attention to the apostle's words: he did not say, "if we have grown up in his death", but "in the pattern of his death". Christ's death is real in him; soul was really separated from body; his body was wrapped in a linen winding sheet. But with you it is the likeness, the pattern of this death and suffering; still you have not received a likeness of salvation, but rather its reality.' The mystery of Christ which was completed in our Lord in all reality in time is, therefore, fulfilled; fulfilled on us first of all in representative, symbolic forms, not purely external ones, but rather images filled with the reality of the new life which is communicated to us through Christ. This special sharing in the life of Christ, both symbolic and real, is what the ancients called mystical;* it is something mediate between a merely outward symbol and the purely real. Thus the Apostolic Constitutions say[1] of the martyr who dies for Christ without baptism 'he dies by experience of Christ, the others in type (τύπος)'. That does not mean that the baptised bears merely an image of Christ's death upon himself, but that in him the Lord's death is fulfilled mystically, that is, in the manner of the sacrament, while the witness in blood shares the complete, natural reality of the Lord's dying. That the sacrament does not simply give the grace of new life, but preserves 'the community of real sufferings by imitation', is what Cyril is emphasizing, in full agreement with St Paul. So we are right to call mysteries those sacred rites which imitate and pass on the mystery of Christ.[2] When St Paul calls the apostles

[1] V, 6, 8.
[2] In this we abstract from the analogy of the ancient mysteries, which is fundamental for terminology. On this matter see, in the next Section, that Christian terminology is in fact (not linguistically) completely intelligible within its own framework. To the texts from St Cyril we may add the detailed and very clear Catecheses of Theodore Mopsuestia, the most important of which I give in J.L.W. 13, 99 ff.

(I Cor. 4, 1) 'stewards of God's mysteries', he means first of all the mystery of Christ which he proclaims, and then, in addition, the sacred actions by which we are taken up and engrafted into this one mystery.

By his passion the Lord became *pneuma*;* accordingly, we too have been filled with *pneuma* through the mystical passion in baptism and the spiritual resurrection which flowed from it: we have become spiritual men. *Pneuma* means the life of godhead, which the Lord gives us, now that he is raised up to it, become it, his human nature uplifted now to God, and his place at the Father's right hand. Possession of the *pneuma* is, according to Peter,[1] Paul,[2] and John,[3] the mark of the Christian[4]. It is expressed in a particularly positive fashion within baptism through the rite of breathing, as the washing primarily expresses purification from sin.*

Through the *pneuma* the Christian is made like Christ, the *pneuma* in person and thereby is himself anointed with this *pneuma*, as Cyril of Jerusalem tells us (Mystagogical Catechesis 3, 1): 'After you were baptised in Christ and had put on Christ, you were formed too in the likeness of the Son of God. Because God predestined that we should have acceptance as his sons, he made us also of one form with Christ's body of glory. Because you are now sharers in Christ you are rightly called christs, anointed ones, and of you God said, "touch not my anointed ones" (Ps. 104, 15). You were anointed as you received the image of the holy *Pneuma*, and everything was done in image upon you, because you are images of the anointed one. He bathed in the river Jordan, and gave the water the good odour of his divinity, so that when he rose out of it, the *pneuma* came bodily upon him, like resting upon like. In just the same way the chrism was given to you as you stepped out of the spring of waters, the off-set of that chrism with which Christ was anointed. But

[1]Acts 2, 38: 'do penance, and be baptised, every one of you in the name of the Lord Jesus, for the remission of your sins and you will receive the gift of the spirit'.

[2]Romans 8, 9: 'You are not in the flesh but in *pneuma*, if God's *pneuma* dwells in you. But if anyone has not Christ's *pneuma*, he is not Christ's.' I Cor. 3, 16: 'do you not know that you are God's temple, and that his *pneuma* dwells in you?'. 12, 3: 'No one can say Jesus is Lord [recognise him as the Christ] except in the *pneuma*.' More precise treatment, ibid, 2, 10–16.

[3]Jn. 3, 24: 'We know that he dwells in us by this token: the *pneuma* he gave to us.' John, too, has the true Spirit recognized in confession of Christ: 'You know God's Spirit by this: every spirit is from God which acknowledges that Jesus Christ has come in the flesh . . .' And 2, 20: 'You have the chrism (the anointing with the Spirit) from the holy one. . . .'

[4]By their common share in the Spirit, all Christians become one body of Christ: 'for in one spirit were all baptised into one body.' (I Cor. 12, 13.)

this is the holy *pneuma* of whom the blessed Isaias spoke in the person of the Lord, "the Spirit of the Lord is upon me, and he has anointed me to bring the gospel to the poor; he had sent me on his business". With no tangible oil or myrrh was Christ anointed at men's hands; the Father who has chosen him out as saviour of the whole world anointed him with the holy Spirit (Acts 10, 38), and the prophet David cried out, "Thy throne, O God, stands firm from everlasting: a wand of uprightness is the sceptre of thy kingdom. Thou didst love justice and hate wrong; therefore, O God, thy God has anointed thee with the oil of joy before all thy companions" (Ps. 44, 7 ff). As Christ was crucified in fact, buried and raised up again, so you gained your high estate at baptism, crucified with him in likening, buried with him so as to rise with him, so is it, too, for you with the chrism. He was anointed with the oil of spiritual gladness, with the *pneuma*, called the oil of joy because it is the spring of joy in spirit. And you were anointed with myrrh, and in this way became co-sharers, companions of Christ.' The Christian is, therefore, a second christ, *pneuma*. Christ is *pneuma* by the hypostatic union with the divine *Logos* who is *pneuma*;* but this union works an upraising of his human nature which is wholly fulfilled and revealed in the resurrection. The Lord came first in the humbled flesh, because his will was to redeem sinners; this flesh had to be nailed to the cross in order that sin and death should die. But in the very moment when sin was brought down on the cross, the slave Jesus, the humbled Son of Man, appeared in the glory of Kyrios and Son of God. The whole God-man is now *pneuma*. *Pneuma Christi* then denotes the whole Lord as glorified: the divine *pneuma* together with the glorification of the man Jesus. If the mere man is christed after the model of the *kyrios* raised up in the *pneuma's* fashion, it means that this man's being is exalted, too, through God's grace, and the in-dwelling of the Trinity which follows upon it.[1] Not as it were the *Logos* alone, for in the redemption and incarnation all three persons act together and Father, Son, Holy Spirit are of one indivisible substance. Therefore we read in John 14, 23: 'if any man love me, he will keep my word, and my Father will love him, and we shall come to him, and take up our abode with him', and verse 26 speaks immediately of the advocate, the Holy Spirit, whom the Father will send in my name.

Through initiation, therefore (baptism and confirmation), man becomes a living member of Christ, a 'christus'. Now he is no *mere* man,

[1]Better, by the in-dwelling of God and the exaltation of human nature which flows from it: both things, created and uncreated grace are not to be separated.

but man transformed, divinised, new-begotten out of God to be God's child.[1] He carries the life of God within him.[2] As a member of the High-Priest, Christ, he is himself *christus*, an anointed one; he is a priest who may sacrifice to God the Father, a sacrifice which through Christ becomes uniquely acceptable and accepted.[3]

There is no religion without sacrifice. Religion is the ordering between God and his creature; God bends down to man, and man climbs up toward God; by his taking it and passing it into his possession God makes the sacrifice holy and consecrates it. If the offerer is stained with sin, and thereby retarded in his sacrifice, the act must become first of all one of reparation. In this case it is carried out first in the form of a purification to make the sacrifice proper acceptable. 'Without bloodshed there is no forgiveness'[4] and no sacrifice of sinful man. The sacrifice made pure by reparation can find its way up to God. The last and most proper offering is man himself: the offering to God of man's free choice of love; this is the only sacrificial gift which does not already belong to God in this fashion.[5] Man wants to go up to God and be healed by him. But where he cannot or will not himself be the sacrifice, he finds a

[1] Jn. 1, 12 f 'to those who received him he gave the power to become God's children, to those who believed his name . . . were begotten of God.' According to 3, 5, the Christian is born anew of water and the Spirit, and what is born of Spirit is Spirit. I Jn. 3, 9: 'no-one who is born of God sins, because God's seed abides in him'; 5, 18: 'we know that no-one who is born of God can sin, but the divine origin protects him and evil does not lay hands on him'. St Paul writes to the Galatians: 3, 26 'you are God's sons by faith in Jesus Christ.' And 4, 4 ff: 'when the fulness of time came, God sent his Son, born of a woman, subject to the law, to pay the price for them who were its subjects, and to give us the acceptance sons have. But that you might be sons (it follows) God has sent the Spirit of his Son into our hearts to cry out, Abba, Father.' Romans 8, 14 ff: 'They who are moved by the Spirit are God's sons, For you have not received the spirit of slavery for fear, but the spirit of acceptance as sons, in which we cry out, "Abba, Father".'

[2] Jn. 1, 4 'In him was life and the life was the light of men.' 6, 57: 'As the living Father sent me and I live through the Father, so he who eats my flesh will live through me.' 11, 25: 'I am the resurrection and the life; the man who believes in me will live, even though he die.' 5, 24 ff: 'The man who hears my word and believes the one who has sent me, has eternal life . . .' I Jo. 1, 1 ff ' . . . of the Word of life . . . life was revealed and we have seen it and given witness to it; we tell you of everlasting life which was with the Father, and was revealed to us . . .'

[3] I Peter 2, 4 ff. 'Coming to him (Christ) you will be formed as living stones into a spiritual dwelling, a holy priesthood, to make spiritual offering well pleasing to God through Jesus Christ. . . .' 'You are a chosen race, a royal priesthood. . . .' Cf Hebrews 13, 15: 'through him we make continual sacrifice of praise to God.'

[4] Heb. 9, 22.

[5] cf M. ten Hompel, *Das Opfer als Selbsthingabe und seine ideale Verwirklichung im Opfer Christi* (1920) 35 ff.

substitute: this was the case with Jews and pagans. In Christianity the primitive idea of sacrifice was restored, when the greatest representative of all mankind, the god-man Jesus Christ, made a total offering of himself to God on the cross.

In God's eyes, Christ is mankind's spokesman; but because at the same time he is God, the Son of God, he is the Father's messenger to mankind. A mere man could have made no sacrifice to please the Father; even in paradise Adam's sacrifice of love was pleasing to God only because the *pneuma* was in him, and gave back to God, in this way what was his. After his sin, man could bring no proper sacrifice.

God, of course, did accept the sacrifice of Abel and the other holy men of the Old Testament, but only in the light of Christ's sacrifice to come. Man could not now go up to God of his own power. God had first to make the way for him, give him reconciliation, come down to him, so that the individual might dare to approach God once more. God's descent came in the incarnation and the sacrifice of Christ. So we read in the Epistle to the Hebrews, 'What the law contains is only the shadow of those blessings which were still to come (i.e. in the new alliance), not the full expression of their reality.' The same sacrifices are offered by the priests of the Old Testament year after year without ceasing, and still the worshippers can never reach, through the law, their full measure of growth. If they could, must not the offerings have ceased before now? There would be no guilt left to reproach the consciences of those who come to worship; they would have been cleansed once for all. No, what these offerings bring with them, year by year, is only a remembrance of sins; but that sins should be taken away by the blood of bulls and goats is impossible. As Christ comes into the world, he says: 'No sacrifice, no offering was thy demand; thou hast endowed me, instead, with a body. Thou hast not found any pleasure in burnt sacrifices, in sacrifices for sin. See then, said I, I am coming to fulfil what is written of me, where thy book lies unrolled; to do thy will, O my God . . . through this will we have been made holy by the offering of the body of Jesus Christ once for all.'[1] Christ therefore has made this sacrifice in his human nature, but with the power godhead gave him. So it was God himself who performed the reconciliation in Christ's sacrifice as St Paul says to us: 'one died for all; all then, died. And he died on behalf of all so that those who live should live no longer for themselves, but for him who died and rose for them . . . so that if any

[1]Heb. 10, 1–10.

one is in Christ he is a thing new made; older things are past (look!), all things have become new. All this from God who has reconciled us to himself through Christ who, in turn, ministers reconciliation to us; in this way, God was in Christ, reconciling the cosmos to himself, not taking into account its faults . . .'[1] At the deepest level, it is God who has offered the sacrifice; for 'God did so love the world that he sent his only-begotten Son into the world', that we might live in him.[2] This was the fashion of his life: 'not that we loved him, but that he loved us, and sent his Son as a sacrifice of reconciliation for our sins'.[3]

How Christ carried out this sacrifice, we have seen when we sketched the economy of it; there, we showed, that this will to sacrifice was accepted and completed through an obedience to death, and the glory and transfiguration of Christ which flowed from it. His rise to the state of kyrios first gives the Lord his consecration as priest. 'He has reached his fulness, and is author of everlasting salvation for all who give him obedience.'[4] 'Through his eternal priesthood he can continually save those who make their way to God through him; he lives forever to make intercession on our behalf.'[5] 'We have such an high priest who has taken his place at the right hand of the throne of majesty, in heaven; one who performs the rites of the holy place and of the real tabernacle, which no man, but rather God has made.'[6]

Because of the inmost oneness of being, and the realm of action following upon it, which grows up between bride and bridegroom, between head and body, it follows that the church must take a share in Christ's sacrifice, in a feminine, receptive way, yet one which is no less active for that. She stands beneath the cross, sacrifices her bridegroom, and with him, herself. But she does so not merely in faith or in some mental act, but rather in a real and concrete fashion, in mystery; she fulfils the 'likening' of that sacrifice through which the Lord offered himself in the presence of earth and heaven, in utter openness, in the total giving of his body, to the Father.* Here again we meet the essential meaning of the mystery of worship: without this mystery, the church would be an offerer without sacrifice, an altar with no gift, a bride cut off from her bridegroom, unconsecrated, knowing no way to the Father.

Then, too, Christ would be priest without people, no high-priest, nor

---

[1]II Cor. 5, 14–19. [2]Jn. 3, 16.
[3]I Jn. 4, 9 f. [4]Heb. 5, 9 f.
[5]Heb. 7, 24 f. [6]Heb. 8, 1–3.

'prince of salvation'.[1] He might not call his members 'brethren' as the apostle has him do: 'the one who sanctifies and the ones who are sanctified are of common origin, all of them; he is not ashamed, then, to own them as his brethren. I will proclaim thy renown, he says, to my brethren; with the assembly around me I will praise thee; and elsewhere he says, "I will put my trust in him", and then, "Here stand I, and the children God has given me". And since these children have an inheritance of flesh and blood, he too shared that inheritance with them. . . .'[2] Christ has gone before us into the holy of holies; 'has become high-priest forever according to the order of Melchisedech'.[3] We must follow him. Over and over again in different ways the oneness of priest and people is emphasised. But as Christ, not by inward devotion alone, but by his own blood,[4] became the minister of the Sanctuary,[5] and a minister all the more exalted as the mediator of the alliance;[6] so, too, his people must make true, outwardly recognisable liturgical sacrifice, From this, too, follows the necessity of the mystery of worship: a visible community can only express its inward oneness and its harmonious action in God's service through a common ritual act. An act common to God and his human community can only be properly carried out in a symbolic action where priesthood (as mediator) takes both God's part and the people's, and gives outward expression by words and gestures to the will of both; thus the invisible action of God upon man is made known through the symbolic action of the priest, as is the deed of the worshipping community in the words and gestures which the priest employs.

These requirements are fulfilled for the Church's sacrifice, the Mass. In it the consecration of the elements by God's deed, which the priest performs in God's power again sets out the sacrificing death of the Lord in *mysterium*. Christ, therefore, offers himself in a sacramental manner: 'in his mystery he suffers for us anew'.[7] But the church 'through the priests' ministry'[8] carries out the mystery and so offers her bridegroom's sacrifice; it is then, at the same time, her sacrifice. It becomes her sacrifice, too, by a most personal participation; mystically engrafted into Christ as his body and spouse the church joins herself by the most intensive self-giving to his offering, so that she becomes one

[1]Heb. 2, 10.   [2]Heb. 2, 11–14; Rom. 8, 29.
[3]Heb. 6, 20.   [4]Heb. 9, 12.
[5]Heb. 8, 2.   [6]Heb. 8, 6.
[7]Gregory the Great, Hom in Evang. 3, 7. J.L.W. 6 (1926), p. 173 f.
[8]*Sacerdotum ministerio*, Council of Trent, Session XXII.

sacrifice with him. Here the mystical Christ (Christ and his church) reveals itself as the true high priest of the new covenant.[1] Here once more we may see the essential and necessary position of the mystery of worship within the mystery of Christ. Without it, the mystery of Christ could not become a reality age after age, from one generation to another, until the whole body shall be saved and its glory revealed with the glory of the head.

We present here a passage on the theme of the mystical body's growth and maturity through the mystery of worship, from the penetrating work of Methodius of Philippi.

'It is entirely consistent with this,[2] that the church should have risen from his (Christ's) flesh and blood; for her sake the Logos left his Father in heaven, and came down to cling to his spouse, and fall asleep in pain, going out of himself by dying freely for her. By this, after he had purified her by bathing, he made the church glorious and without spot, to receive the spiritual, holy seed which, with mild words, he sows and plants in the mind's deep places; but the church takes it, in woman's fashion, and forms it, to bring forth virtue and let it grow up. Thus is carried out the word, "increase and multiply yourselves", when she grows in stature and loveliness each day, through contact and communion with the Logos, who, even now (at the memorial of the suffering), comes down upon us, and passes out of himself.

'In no other way could the church receive the faithful and bear them through the bath of new birth. Christ had to divest himself so that we might take hold of him again when his sufferings were represented; he had so to die again, come down from heaven, and, to join himself to the church his spouse, to make her able to gain strength from his side; thus all who have their foundation in him, who are born of the bath, were to grow, by increasing of his bone and his flesh, that is to say, of his holiness and glory. Flesh and bone of wisdom are the right names for prudence and virtue, but they come from the Spirit of truth, the advocate who gives to the illumined new birth and everlasting life. But

---

[1]The co-offering of the faithful rests first of all on the objective sacramental engrafting of every Christian into the body of Christ by baptism. What the body does, the members do in company with it. The more conscious this participation is, the more deeply it is experienced, the more intensive the participation. This explains the necessity of active participation in the liturgical celebration and in its external form; the external strengthens what is within. See Section iii.

[2]Namely with the allegorical explanation of the first human pair as Christ and his church.

it is impossible that anyone should share in the holy *pneuma* and be called a member of Christ if the *Logos* did not first come down upon him and fall asleep in holy distraction, so as to bring him once more to the resurrection from sleep, and make him able to share, filled with the *pneuma*, in the refreshment and renewal of youthfulness. This *pneuma* of truth, sevenfold, according to the prophet, is called the *Logos*' right hand; God takes from him, after the holy distraction, that is the incarnation and the passion, and from him makes the helpers, the souls which are bound up to him and entrusted to him.'[1]

From the ritual memorial of the passion, therefore, the church is always growing, is being filled by the *pneuma*, is growing up to the full age of Jesus Christ.

But its sacrificial being does not exhaust the mystery of the eucharist; it has a side which is more sacramental in the narrower sense. The sacrifices of the Old Testament were partly offerings of food, presented to God and consecrated by this fact; those who shared the communion of the sacrifice ate them and so were themselves raised to communion with God. The sacrifice of the New Testament is also a food-offering, but in a much higher, more *spiritual* sense. Christ has given himself as the food of the world, the bread of life[2] and the drink of eternal life.[3] 'If you do not eat the flesh of the Son of Man and drink his blood, you have no life in you. The man who eats my flesh and drinks my blood has everlasting life.[4] The incarnate *Logos* is really the nourishment of the world, because through his utterance and his *pneuma* he gives it life beyond nature and preserves that life for it. Christ has made this fact a mystery, too, because he wanted to express the real union between himself and the church in a communion of flesh and blood in the most concrete fashion possible. The explanation which he gives in John 6 becomes ever more 'mysterious' and sacramental as it progresses. Its darkness becomes light, through its concrete and holy fulfilment at the Last Supper, when the Lord gave his body and blood to the disciples in the forms of bread and wine, that is to say in the form of sacrificial food. This makes clear that not only the incarnate *Logos* but the *Logos* murdered is the world's food. If we want to express that in ritual, there is no better or simpler way than the one which the Lord chose, namely to give his sacrificial body and blood to his disciples in the form of food and

---

[1]Symposium 3, 8: cf J.L.W. 6 (1926) p. 144 ff.
[2]Jn. 6, 35 and 50 ff.   [3]Jn. 4, 14 and 9, 37.
[4]Jn. 6, 53 ff.

drink, and so to show in the most palpable way that the *Kyrios*, killed and raised up on high, is the inward power of his church which penetrates its whole being, fills it with the force of God's own life.

The three mysteries we have mentioned, baptism, confirmation, eucharist as food are the stages of complete engrafting into the body of Christ. Baptism cleanses from sin by plunging us into the cross; confirmation breathes the new god-life of *pneuma* into us, and communion strengthens and preserves it, makes the members grow up to their full measure in the body. They form, then, Christian initiation, the beginning of Christian life. Those who are so consecrated to it can go on immediately with the greatest act of the mystical Christ, his offering of himself and his love to the father. Through this sharing in his act, the Christian grows once more into the body; the blood purifies him again and again, the Spirit of resurrection enlivens him and strengthens him, while the sacrificial food incorporates him more and more fully into Christ, the Lord. These three mysteries are therefore the most important and most necessary for the life of the church and each Christian.

Still, the body of Christ is a living organism, not a dead heap of similar atoms: it has a variety of members with different functions, both in its final form and—which is of more concern to us—in the accomplishing those of its tasks on earth which will come to an end with the end of this world's time, that is to say when the whole body has grown to the fullness of its age and it will have no more need of human works.[1] In the first place the members need a representation on earth of the invisible head: men—for woman represents the church's bridal nature— who will act for Christ in a special fashion as leaders, teachers, priests. The mystery of priestly ordination assimilates the men Christ has called to those characteristics of his. The *pneuma* comes down upon them in a marvellous fashion, and through the laying on of hands by bishops, successors of the apostles, acts upon them; this rite represents and carries on the connexion with the apostles, and hence with Christ himself. In addition to those in authority the church also has other men and women—here sex makes no difference—who are to shine out before the whole body as models of holiness and consecration to God. They are to put on in a special way the likeness to Christ, crucified and risen in *pneuma*. Hence, the mysteries of the consecration of monks[2] and of virgins, and of the abbot and abbess as leaders of this life.

[1]Cf Eph. 4, 11–16.
[2]Cf J.L.W. 5, p. 1 f on Solemn Monastic Profession.

These states were counted from the beginning as states of immediate consecration to God. In the course of time they were marked by an act of ritual consecration; they retained their character as spirit-informed men, with, of course, no place in the hierarchy. The meaning of what they did was total consecration to God. The consecrated widows come into this category too. In these dedications a part was also played by the hierarchy of heaven: it is as the Church's spiritual states that these men and women are called: apostles, martyrs, confessors, virgins, widows. As the office of the church shows, they become the names of classes of saints in the choirs of heaven.[1]

With the state of marriage we return to this *aion*, for 'the children of this world marry and are given in marriage; but those who are found worthy to attain the other world, and resurrection from the dead, take neither wife nor husband'.[2] But it, too, is wonderfully exalted in the new alliance, for now it is an image of the spiritual marriage in the new covenant between Christ and his church, just as Paradise pointed towards this alliance yet to come. When, in Ephesians, St Paul gives Christ and his church as the model for Christian married people he says, 'this mystery is a great one; I speak of Christ and the church'.[3] The primaeval mystery is, therefore, the spiritual bond between Christ and his *ecclesia*, and the marriage of two Christians is a grace-giving image of that bond. The sacrament of marriage, too, has its ultimate meaning and its blessing from the mystery of Christ; and the same mystery works its effects in all the other reaches of life. Paul says, 'the unbelieving husband is sanctified in the wife and the unbelieving wife in her fellow Christian; otherwise your children would be unclean, but now they are clean';[4] in the last instance baptism will heal them. Sickness and death require a special measure of the strength of Christ's grace. 'Is anyone sick among you, let him call the priests of the church, and they will pray over him, anointing him with oil in the Lord's name; and the prayer of faith will save the sick man, and the Lord will rouse him, and if he have sinned, it will be forgiven him.'[5] For the sinners who are not ill there is also forgiveness of sins in the power of the mystery of Christ; no second baptism, but rather the return of the Spirit which had been lost, through the laying on of the bishop's hands.[6] Nor does the

---

[1]High regard for episcopal office is shown in that confessors are distinguished as bishops and other confessors.

[2]Lk. 20, 35.   [3]Eph. 5, 32.

[4]Cor. 7, 14.   [5]James 5, 14 ff.

[6]The practice today is for absolution with the priest's upraised hand.

dead man lack the helping and saving power of the church's mysteries; according to ancient custom in the church he is anointed and prayed for; the eucharist is offered for him.[1] It is not possible to show here how the mystery goes about its work in the many rites and prayers which accompany every step of the life of Christian man and community, and bring the *pneuma* of Christ into every sphere and relationship of living. Christians know this from their own experience.

This short exposition should show that the religion of the gospel, the piety of the New Testament, and the worship of the Church cannot exist without the mystery of worship. We are to think of liturgy (λειτουργία) in its pure and ancient meaning: not an extension of aesthetically-minded ritualism, not ostentatious pageantry, but the carrying out, the making real of the mystery of Christ in the new alliance throughout the whole church, in all centuries; in it her healing and glory are made fact. This is what we mean when we say that liturgical mystery is the most central and most essential action of the Christian religion.

ii *Mystery and Ritual types*

The New Testament taught us that Christianity is Christ's good news; it is a mystery, which contains the incarnation, the invisible God's visible appearance among us, the act of redemption on the cross, culminating in the resurrection through which the Lord showed us his glory, not indeed to the whole world, but to those few witnesses 'whom God had chosen out',[2] and through them to the Church (*ecclesia*). The parousia at the end of time will end this plan of salvation. In the time between, the church lives by faith and in the mysteries of Christ's worship. These mysteries are a working out and an application of Christ's mystery. God, who revealed himself in the man Christ, acts now, after this man has been glorified, acts now properly for the first time. He works through Christ the high-priest and the usual ordering of the Church's means of grace in the mystery of worship, which is nothing else than the God-man acting on earth from age to age. For this reason, it, like him, shares God's majesty and action and is hidden beneath symbols,[3] taken from the world, which both hide and point to

---

[1] Cf *Altchristliches in der Totenliturgie* Lit. Ztschrift 3 (1930/31) 18–26. In Dionysius the Aeopagite, burial belongs to the mysteries.

[2] Acts 10, 40 f.

[3] Cf Irenaeus of Lyons, *Contra Haereses* IV, 18, 5 'As the bread which comes from the earth receives God at the epiclesis (calling upon his name) and is ordinary bread no longer but eucharist, with two elements, earthly and heavenly; so our bodies when they take the eucharist are corruptible no longer, but possess the hope of everlasting life.' (Cf V 2, 3.)

its reality. Thus it is possible that the Lord, though eternally glorified in heaven and visible to all, should be still hidden in the world, and go on revealing the whole strength of his glory. The Lord's manner of presence in the mystery therefore, holds a position between that in his life on earth before the resurrection, and his glorified life in heaven: the divine power is fully in action, yet faith must be there to see it; there is not yet simple vision. 'We go our way in faith, not seeing.'[1] So in the mysteries is fulfilled what we heard: 'blessed are they who see not, and yet believe'.[2] On this St Leo the Great comments, 'In order that we might share in this blessedness our Lord put an end to his bodily presence among us. First of all he performed what was necessary for the preaching of the gospel and the mysteries of the New Testament; then he rose up to heaven before his disciples, forty days after he had come back from the tomb. There he will remain, at the Father's right hand, until the time is past which God has allotted for his children to be multiplied, and comes again in the flesh in which he rose, to judge the living and the dead. What was visible in our redeemer has passed over into the mysteries; and, that faith may be nobler and more firm, after vision came teaching, whose influence the faithful are to follow, illumined by the rays of light from heaven.'[3] The Saviour then, adapts himself entirely through the mystery to his church's state; and by so doing, he carries out the great saving design, the *economy*, which was not meant merely for those who walked with him on earth, but for all generations, and all ages until the end of this world's time. The church still walks in faith's darkness, not the light of vision; yet, she is already redeemed, she already possesses the 'pledge of the Spirit',[4] lives 'in Christ'[5] glorified; she is his body, and his bride. Therefore she gives herself to him with all the high-priestly strength he has given her; but under the veil of the symbols. She is not yet utterly redeemed and united inseparably with God; she has still in her members to fight with sin and with the world; she is not recognized, but persecuted, and she must weep at the number of her own children who fall. She is more like the crucified Lord than him risen and carried up to glory, although she bears within herself the riches which are the reflection of it; riches which flash out secretly from time to time. So the *mysterium* also shines with God's own

[1]II Cor. 5, 7 cf I Cor. 13, 12.   [2]Jn. 20, 29.
[3]Sermo 74, 2 Migne 54, 398; cf J.L.W. 8 (1928) p. 154.
[4]Romans 8, 23.
[5]The well-known formula of St Paul. Cf Wikenhauser, *Die paulinische Christusmystik* (1928).

jewels, but hides them beneath a veil which at once covers and portrays them; what it portrays is first of all the cross of Christ, his dying and his blood, and through these the glory which comes after. The mystery is like the stones on an ancient jewelled cross, which do not change its shape, yet clothe the bareness of the wood with loveliness. Baptism points first of all to the killing of the old man; the fragrance of its ointment breathes the good smell of resurrection. The mass is a memorial of Christ's death; his body, sacrificed and his blood poured out are shown to us. But that this body and blood should become food and drink for life is fruit and symbol of the resurrection to everlasting life. Through these mysteries the church takes her share in the passion of Christ, the passion by which 'he died to sin', and through this dying she takes her share in his life which 'he lives for God'.[1] Through the cross she is filled with the *pneuma*, made holy, brought to glory, deified.

The mystery, then, becomes a bridal gift which is of extraordinary fitness for the church; it is her espousals, her very life which the mystery gives her, a deep communion with Christ in living and acting. Here is the fulfilment of the mystical marriage of which St Paul sees a shadowy image in human marriage: the mystery which is completed to full measure 'in Christ and the church'.[2]

Thus we come upon another light shed on the need for the mystery, from the church's point of view. As the spouse of the new spiritual Adam it is she who receives of him, and yet is 'like him';[3] she shares in his work in the cultivation of the very gift she has received; she makes it a thing of beauty, and gives it back to her lover. The church has nothing of her own, for 'what hast thou which thou hast not received?'[4] Even after Christ's great sacrificial deed she could bring nothing new to the Father; Christ fulfilled the sacrifice for all time: 'through one gift of sacrifice he has perfected forever those to be made holy';[5] 'there is no other offering for sin'.[6] Over and over again the New Testament teaches us that Christ completes the divine plan of salvation, and the new *aion* is here among us[7]; after him there is no new kingdom, no new sacrifice or healing. His sacrifice was the evening offering of the world, and his resurrection the dawn of a new and everlasting morning.[8] Yet the church still wants to

[1]Rom. 6, 10.   [2]Eph. 6, 22–32.
[3]Gen. 2, 18.   [4]I Cor. 4, 17.
[5]Heb. 10, 14.   [6]Heb. 10, 26.
[7]Cf for example Heb. 1, 2; 9, 26. I Peter 2, 20.
[8]This is the mystical sense of the supper and of Christ's dying in the evening and rising in the morning.

give testimony of her love, through a sacrifice; she wants to make the gift of her love to the Father, in a tangible, symbolic form, now, while she is still a pilgrim; she will be doing, not merely taking something. For this, again, she has the mysteries and in them she can express her love and meaning: their symbolic elements are taken from the earth,[1] just as their words are a part of human speech; these sacred acts are men's acts, acts the church can make its own, can perform again and again,[2] surround with warmth and beauty; in this way she turns them into eloquent signs of her own mind's devotion. Yet, in all of this, she does not separate herself from her bridegroom, for from him she receives continually the heart of these mysteries, and it is his life she lives in them.

Ever more clearly, then, we see that the rite-form 'mystery', that definite form of worship which the word and concept *mysterium* denote, is wholly necessary in the worship of the new alliance; it is not merely for the exterior service which is due to God from a visible community, but also, precisely for the inmost and essential self-gift to God which is the last end of all Christian worship. For in this new alliance God has revealed himself to be love, and love it is he seeks, not honour, from his creatures. A Christ-mysticism is the real centre of New Testament ritual, the physical or realistic uniting of the church, as the body or the bride, with Christ the glorified God-man, and with him to the trinity, so that God is all in all.[3] The other two forms (εἴδη, species) those of prayer and sacrifice, meet in the New Testament in the mystery form. Only conjoined to its head can the body of Christ pray in *pneuma*;[4] the only sacrifice the Church can make is that which Christ, her head and saviour, has made.

Every act of worship, every act towards God under the new covenant, is joined essentially with the mystery, and is stamped by it with the mark of Christ; God receives nothing without this mark, under the new alliance. The mystery belongs to those unspeakable riches which God has given us in Christ. The old covenant had no mysteries;* in it God had not yet appeared as man among us, not yet died for us on the cross;

---

[1] Note 3, page 27.
[2] *Frequentare* in liturgical prayers.
[3] I Cor. 15, 28.
[4] Romans, 8, 26 f: 'the Spirit comes to the aid of our weakness when we know not what we ought to pray for, to pray as we ought the Spirit himself intercedes for us with unutterable groanings, and God who can read our hearts, knows well what the Spirit's intent is; for indeed it is according to the mind of God that he makes intercession for the saints.'

the other hemisphere was not yet open to man, for Christ had not yet come to open it. Fear still ruled, the law of love had not yet been preached. The everlasting covenant of *agape*, that love of God's, with no works as its condition, was not yet formed; there was only a bond for a certain time, built on the law. The shared work of God and man belongs to the mystery; its author can only be a God-man, and this work gives entrance into the eternal, divine, life, here already 'in promise', while its fullness is reserved for the time to come. The mystery gives a most intimate, most real union with God; the Father begets, the *Logos* joins himself to us as bridegroom; *Agape*, God's own love, is the mark of this mystical union. Only the new alliance could bring the mystery and through it reveal the inmost heart of God, his love.

Jewish worship, of course, had the forms of 'memorial' along with prayer and sacrifice. Because God showed himself to the Jews in historical events, these events were to be kept continually before the people's minds; first of all, the liberation from Egypt, upon which the existence of Israel as God's sacred people turned, was celebrated in the annual feast of the Passover. God's prescriptions were carried in exact ritual: the paschal lamb eaten in travelling clothes; the history read recalling how they left the land where they were slaves. So Israel's salvation and the founding of God's people was celebrated each year in ritual, and God's preserving of Israel in the promised land secured anew.[1]

But the passover use was not properly a mystery because it was related first of all to human events, and a human deliverance.* It was the Pasch of Christ, his bloody death, which saved the world from its sins and fed it with food of everlasting life, god-life. On the eve of the earth's pasch, the saviour made of this pasch a complete mystery; he anticipated his death in the mystical rite, and made food of his sacrificed body, gave his blood as the foundation of a covenant. Here an historic event was celebrated but one which had its end beyond time, in God, in the passage from this *aion* to the world to come. It was not only an action of God's upon his people, but an action he carried out among them in human form. Now men were given the power of imitating and following

[1]On the paschal meal see Strack-Billerbeck *Kommentar* IV, 1 (1928) 40 ff, esp. p. 68: 'In every generation man is obliged to act as if he had come out of Egypt, for it says, "for the sake of what Jahwe did for me as I came out of Egypt" ' (Ex. 13, 18). (Pes, 10, 5). Billerbeck comments (p. 69): 'Here is the plainest expression of the idea that the paschal meal is meant to be a memorial meal.'

in what God made man had done among them, and so of sharing in his life by means of their own concrete deed.

This pasch of Christ was, therefore, something completely his own, with no expression in the old covenant; hence it was such an abomination to Judaism, with its own single mind. The Jews, like all Semitic peoples thought of God as a powerful, terrible ruler, separated from mankind by an unbridgeable gap, whom one approached fearful and adoring; here was no room for a close relationship. Even the language of these peoples could not express the new god-life of the new alliance.* But God, in his providence, had seen to the growth of certain religious forms which, while not approaching closely to Christian reality, could offer words and forms to express this new, unheard-of thing in a way open to men's understanding.

The Indo-germanic peoples in their striving for deeper union with God had gradually fashioned richer and more refined forms of worship. These, particularly in the Hellenistic age, following the campaigns of Alexander the Great, entered a period of fruitful mixing of Greek and near Eastern ideas, and led to the mystery cults. This synthesis, which in many respects was to give its language and form to the coming Christianity—the Gospel is written in its common language, and dogma, too, used its superb power of expression—developed the ritual-form *mystery* to its classical height. Its fundamental idea was participation in the lives of the gods, who in some way or other had appeared in human form, and taken part in the pain and happiness of mortal men. The believer acted with them by sharing their suffering and deeds portrayed in the rite, and performed in it once more by ritual imitation. Thereby he entered into an intimacy with them which was expressed through various images taken from human life; he became a member of the race of gods.[1] This gave him the assurance that after death he would not share the general fate of mortals in Hades' darkness, but attain the blessedness of light; already on earth it cut him off from the mass of uninitiated, and made him a 'holy man', a consecrated person; sometimes it gave moral impulses as well. The *Mystai* formed among themselves a close, sacred community, under a selected, ruling priesthood. Worship in this community was carried out with rich and dramatic symbolism in which the divine actions were performed in a hieratic and formal manner with a rich use of natural symbolism. We hear for example that the high-point of the Eleusinian mysteries was the showing to the μύσται of a newly-

[1]In Eleusis for example.

cut ear of corn: a symbol of the newly burgeoning life, to men striving for it, a pledge of life after death.[1]

We may not, of course, carry over our elaborate concepts of Christian symbolism into the ancient mysteries. They remained the prisoners of unredeemed nature, in the slavery of the 'world's elements' as St Paul says of a Jewish-hellenistic cult;[2] they did not lead to the supernatural life of the true God. They were only a shadow, in contrast to the Christian mysteries; but they were a longing, 'a shadow of things to come'; the body whose shadow they cast was 'the body of Christ'[3] which showed itself beforehand in the types of the old Testament too. An analogy existed for them, as it did for the whole of nature and super-nature, and so they were able to lend words and forms to the mysteries of Christ which belonged to that supernature. They did not give exist-ence or content; how, indeed, were the weak and poor elements of the world[4] to attain of themselves the mystery of Christ? But they made it possible to give a body to the new and unconceived elements of the New Testament's revelation. When St Paul speaks of the 'things wrapped in silence for the ages' or of the 'hidden mystery', everyone in the ancient world knew immediately what this was: the familiar language of the mysteries, its purpose to make clearer to them, that as these mysteries were surrounded by a terrible majesty which claimed reverence, so, too, God's saving design came out of the hidden depths of his vast silences; and that these silences were now revealed. The whole new way of wor-ship in the Christian community could no longer be expressed in the old language of Jewish or pagan ritual. We have only to call up the picture: on the one hand, the vast temple, with its huge altars, covered with the blood of slaughtered animals and smoky from countless burnt offerings, served by a throng of priests to kill the animals; choirs and shouts of the people: here was prayer and sacrifice in the old fashioned way, a reverence to all-powerful divinity. On the other hand, the Christian community without temple or altar, in simple houses around a table, with bread and wine. A leader says the *eucharistia*, the memorial renewed of Jesus crucified and risen; a family meal is held, bringing the community together. Was this cult of any kind in the ancient sense? Yes, said the Christians; here was the only true sacrifice: the mystical Christ

[1]For details, my *Liturgie als Mysterienfeier* (1923) also *Mysterium in Gesammelte Arbeiten laacher Mönche* (1926) particularly p. 29 ff.

[2]Col. 2, 8 and 20. Jewish cult is slavery to the elements of the world. Gal. 4, 3 and 9.

[3]Col. 2, 17.   [4]Gal. 4, 9.

sacrificing with and for his church, filling her with his Spirit. This is where the official ritual language of the Jews and pagans gave up; this mystical common work of Christ and the church could, if at all, and then only to a limited degree, find expression in the language of the mysteries, purified of everything merely natural, and made resplendent. In any case we observe that even quite early expressions from the mysteries are used for the Christian mystery; Christian writers like Justin Martyr, Tertullian, even Cyprian, note with astonishment the analogy of the mysteries, and comment on them. Moreover this takes place at the same time as the church held these mysteries in detestation —it was a period of their flowering—and fought them with all her power. From the peace of Constantine, the church's triumph over paganism, the language of the ancient mysteries was used even more unhesitatingly to express the unfathomable content of what she herself possessed, as far as this was possible at all; indeed many ancient forms and customs were taken over to enrich and adorn Christian simplicity. The gold and silver of Egypt, to use one of the fathers' favourite images, was melted down to embellish the vessels of the church.

In the course of time, the language of the mysteries, as a glance into the Roman Missal[1] shows us, became so much the church's property, that all consciousness of its ancient origin was lost. Who thinks of the word sacrament as resting in last analysis on the language of the ancient mysteries?[2] But this is no simple loss of memory through the usualness of the thing, but rather the consequence of the fact that Christianity is of its own very essence, as we saw above, a mystery religion, and the mystery language its own most rightful possession. The ancient church lived in mystery, and needed to construct no theory about it.*

The situation became different after the beginning of modern times, and the growth and development of modern thought which entered into ever sharper opposition to the thinking of the church. Ancient thought, considered as a whole, had a great reverence for all being: the individual felt himself to be a member of the great cosmos, and willingly submitted to its order. The self-seeker was taken for a rebel; his deed was ὕβρις which brought down the anger of the gods. Behind the visible world the

---

[1]On the ancient Roman sacramentaries whose texts have been partly preserved in the Roman Missal, Cf J.L.W. 2 (1922) p. 18 ff. For the mystery language of the Greek rites see P. Hendrix *Der Mysteriencharakter der byzant. Liturgie* (Byzant. Ztschrift 30 (1929) p. 333–339).

[2]Cf *Theol. Revue* 24 (1925), 41–47 and J.L.W. 8 (1928), p. 225–232 where the word *sacramentum* is discussed, and the passage from Greek μυστήριον to Latin *sacramentum*.

deep sight of ancient man saw a higher kingdom of spirit and godhead, of which the things we see are symbols; reflected reality, and at the same time mediators and bearers of spiritual things. Ancient thinking was at once concrete, because concerned with objects, and spiritual, because these did not remain confined to material objects. To men like these, it did not seem difficult to believe that God could communicate his life through symbols, or that their own religious acts could leap up into the circle of God's life; it was no different whether they conceived these things as more cosmic or as more spiritual; in either case it was a symbolic action which rose to the height of the god's mode of living. The symbolic, strength-giving rites of the mysteries were real for the ancients; when the church of Christ entered the world she did not end, but rather fulfilled their way of thinking.[1] Christ, of course, put nature out of its exclusive rulership, when he revealed God, as transcending the universe, taught us of the Spirit of life, and gave it to us. In his preaching, beside the community is the irreplaceable value of the individual soul. But he left the unconditional rule of God and the community all their pride of place; he gave them their final reason and highest development. It was symbolism which was sanctified and divinized when the *Logos* appeared in human flesh, and 'we saw the glory of God in the face of Christ'.[2] It cannot seem strange to us, then, when at his going away, Christ leaves the mysteries as signs of his divine presence, or when John, deepest of the evangelists, in his 'Spirit-informed' gospel,[3] makes so much of them. On the other hand it is also an historical truth that the Hellenes sometimes found it easier to grasp and to grasp more deeply the truth of the gospel than did the Jews with their purely Semitic, imageless, legal thinking. The Christianity of the ancient world appears to us as the fulfilment and glorification of what Greco-Roman antiquity was.

It became something quite different in the Germanic peoples who had given themselves to Christianity. A new kind of thinking arose when they received the culture of antiquity.* In it man was a lone individual, cut loose from the divine wholeness, moving always towards making himself his own midpoint, constructing for himself his own law and his own world, with no God outside him as an over-lord, no God

---

[1] Cf Mt. 5, 17. For the relationship of ancient culture to Christian worship cf J.L.W. 3, (1923) 1, ff. Also Chapter III.

[2] II Cor. 4, 6.

[3] Clement of Alexandria in Eusebius *Historia Ecclesiastica* VI, 14, 7.

with whom the creature enters into real relations. It followed immediately from this that the things of nature become subjective. They could at best be regarded as arbitary images; images, that is, of human, subjective apprehension; they were emptied of objective, independent value, and could no longer convey God's power. How this destroying, atomising notion took God out of the world and brought down every kind of community, we need not set out in detail; everyone with any vision can see now with dismay where Europe and the world she influences have come, thanks to individualism, old fashioned liberalism and Marxism.[1] The Catholic church has done something miraculous by holding fast to the cosmos of God's values in the midst of general chaos and by keeping for us, in the mystery of worship, symbols full of God's true power and presence. The liturgical renewal in our day is nothing but a new recognition and stress upon these values in the church, and an attempt to make them once more the common property of all the faithful. For there is no doubt that something of man-centred ideas has come into the minds of many Christians, and that this has gradually shown itself, in the life of faith, as rationalism, and in the life of piety as a tendency to introspective self-indulgence. Prayer has been moving away from consciousness of the mystical body of Christ, falling into the isolated feeling and thinking of the 'God-seeking' individual; sacrifice has been taken for nothing more than a mental attitude, and given 'ascetic' value, if not completely subordinated to external activity. The mystery itself, with its objective ordering of things according to God and real union with him disappeared beneath a mass of more or less personal devotional exercises which left more freedom to individual feeling. *Devotio*, a word which to the ancients[2] meant the church's worship, became the devotion of a purely interior state of individual consciousness. This modern spirit pushed its way even into the domain of theology, despite its dogmatic safeguards, and showed itself in a weakening of the great, deep thinking of the older theology, emphasizing man, his reason and his self-rule, to the detriment of God, Christ, church and sacrament. It is quite understandable, then, that the mystery teaching, as the logical outcome (in the sphere of worship and its mystical insight) of the old notions of faith, should be considered by many theologians, to be a foolish, unfounded, and even dangerous doctrine; rejected and fought by them as

[1] Cf Ch. I.
[2] A. Daniels, *Devotio* J.L.W. 1, p. 40 ff.

a deceitful *fata morgana,* it is yet championed by the followers of the old theology who take the Fathers and Aquinas as their models.[1]

This makes it clear that the renewal and revival of the traditional teaching is not due to a whim for touching up long out-dated ideas, nor to aestheticism, or some other arbitrary fancy; it proceeds necessarily from the spiritual state of our time. After the ebb and failure of anthropocentrism, once more the tide of a deeper divine life begins, a striving for God as he really is, for his dreadful majesty revealing itself in the New Testament, not merely as terror as it did in the Old, but as the deepest, incomprehensible love: the abyss of love which would plunge us into itself. This longing to penetrate once again the whole of life with God's lively Spirit, not merely at the 'times of devotion' but in all being and action, is the response to the mystery; its very name shows that it denotes the inconceivable, the power of God's action which surpasses all thinking. Here man can only tremble; not in reverence and terror only, but in love.

New ideas always live first of all in small circles. In this case they first grow out of the heart of the church; but it is surely a work of providence, too, that even in the world outside the church, de-christianized, a new kind of thinking gradually rises. The spirit of rationalism, of self-sufficient science, is more powerful than ever in

[1]For details I note the most important references. J. B. Umberg S.J. assembles the doubts of many theologians in his articles on 'Mystery-piety?' *Ztschrift für Askese und Mystik* 1 (1926) p. 351–366, and 'Mystery-Presence' *Ztschrift für kath. Theologie* 52 (1928) p. 357–400. His operational base is the difficulty, in the mystery-teaching, of conceiving how Christ's past saving act should become present; this is supposed to be philosophically impossible. Yet the difficulty is ill-conceived, because the presence here brought to be is not a natural and historical, but sacramental one. For the notion of sacramental presence cf particularly Vonier's book, *A Key to the Doctrine of the Eucharist* 1925. My answer to Umberg in *Bonner Ztschrift f. Theologie und Seelsorge* 4, 1927, p. 101–117 and J.L.W. 6, 113–204, 8, 145–224, where I seek to show the propriety of the mystery-idea from scripture, patristic tradition and dogmatic theology. The teaching of tradition is further given in J.L.W. 13, 99–171. Gebhard Rohner shows correspondence to Thomistic teaching in *Divus Thomas* (Freiburg) 8, p. 1–17 and 145–174. Some French Jesuits near to Thomism have given the ideas friendly treatment, the patrologists Jules Lebreton and J. de Séguier in *Nouvelle Rev. de Théol.* 61 (1929) p. 289–299, where they attempt to prove the thesis from the Thomistic notion of transubstantiation. Of course it is always well to speak cautiously of proof, as we are here in the realm of the *mysterium stricte dictum.* I have replied to the work of Joseph Dillersberger, *Eine neue Messopfertheorie?* (*Theologie u Glaube,* 22, p. 511–88), which accepts the thesis with some essential differences, in the same periodical (23, p. 351–367). More literature in the literature section of J.L.W. under 'Mass' (Fourth section of the reviews in each volume). B. Neunheuser gives an introductory survey of the speculative work in this area over the last few years: *Lit. Leben* 2, 1935, p. 189–217.*

the masses, but among the better-educated there is the dawn of strivings to new consciousness of symbolism, to a grasp of the need for depth. Mankind today is sick with the rationalism of exact science and longs once more for the symbols of God's world. It can find them, where they have always remained, in Christ's church, where his mystery is proclaimed by the true God and shows the way to him. The church's faithful, however, must learn once more the greatness of their treasures; they must cleanse away the rust of neglect, and let them shine once again in the light which love and knowledge brings to bear, so that they may show the world once more the only true and saving mysteries.

The recent popes have called once more for active sharing in the mysteries of worship;[1] there is the flowing spring of Christ's life. This active sharing will only then be really and truly fulfilled when the Liturgy is known again for what it is at the deepest level: the mystery of Christ and the Church.*

iii *Mystery and Liturgy*

Christ's mystery in God's revelation in the saving action of his incarnate Son and the redemption and healing of the church. It continues after the glorified God-man has returned to his Father, until the full number of the church's members is complete; the mystery of Christ is carried on and made actual in the mystery of worship. Here Christ performs his saving work, invisible, but present in Spirit and acting upon all men of good-will.[2] It is the Lord himself who acts this mystery; not as he did the primaeval mystery of the Cross, alone, but with his bride, which he won there, his church;[3] to her he has now given all his treasures; she is to hand them on to the children she has got of him. Whoever has God for his father must, since the incarnation, have the church for his mother.[4] As the woman was formed in paradise from the side of the first Adam, to be a helpmate, like to him[5], the church is formed from the side of Christ fallen asleep on

---

[1]Cf J. Pinsk in *Lit. Zeitschrift* 3, p. 63.

[2]Lk. 2, 14.

[3]Eph. 5, 14 ff.

[4]Cf St Cyprian, *de Unitate Ecclesiae* 5 f. We are born of the church, drink her milk, are enlivened by her Spirit. . . . She keeps us for God, leads those she had born to his kingdom. The man who cuts himself off from the church and joins an adulteress is separated from the church's promise. He will not attain Christ's reward, if he deserts Christ's church. He is a stranger, an uninitiate, a foreigner. No one can have God for his father who does not have the church for his mother.

[5]Gen. 2, 18.

the cross to be his companion and helper in the work of redemption. At the same time, the fathers teach us[1] the mysteries flow in water and blood from the Lord's side; the church was born from Christ's death-blood and the mystery with it; church and mystery are inseparable. This is the last ground for the fact that the mystery of worship becomes liturgy.

The Greek word Liturgy[2] originally meant the act of an individual in the service of the city; for example fitting up a ship for war, or sponsoring a choir for the tragedies in honour of Dionysus; service generally, and in particular the service of God in public worship. In this sense it is used by Old and New Testament. Thus, Zacharias, the father of John the Baptist, performed his liturgy in the temple.[3] St Clement of Rome speaks in his letter to the Corinthians (40 ff) of the liturgy of the Old Testament which he puts before them as the model for the service of the New. And if in the New Testament the whole of life is sacred and a service of God, the fathers' directions have particular application to the common worship of the Christian community. The rulers of this community 'perform liturgy' for it;[4] they conduct it in the service of God, particularly in his worship. The layman, too, performs his liturgy: the high-priest has received his liturgy, the priest his proper place, the Levites have each their special duties: 'the layman is bound by the prescriptions for the people. Every one of us, brethren, is to please God in the place God has appointed for him, with a good conscience and due dignity, not going over the bounds of his own liturgy'.[5] Here the liturgical order of the temple is carried over into Christian ways; in Hebrews[6] Christ himself is named

---

[1]As one of many we present Augustine's *Tractatus in Joannem* 120, 2: 'it is a pregnant word the evangelist has used; he does not say the soldier thrust into his side, or wounded him in his side, or anything else, but that he opened his side. Thus, so to speak, the doors of life were to be opened through which the church's mysteries proceed, without which no one goes into the life which is true life. This blood was poured out for the remission of sins, this water was preparation for salvation's cup; it made the cleaning water and the good drink. An image of it was the door which Noah made in the side of the ark; through it the animals were to enter, which were not to die in the flood: they signified the church. Therefore the first woman was made from the side of a sleeping man and called life, and mother of the living. She signified a great good thing, before the great woe of sin. And the second Adam fell asleep here on the Cross, with head bowed, so that his spouse might be formed from what flowed out of his side. . . .'

[2]λειτουργία—old Attic λῃϊτουργία: λάος, ἔργον: public work, public service.

[3]Luke 1, 23.   [4]I Clement 44, 4.

[5]I Clement 40, 5–41.   [6]I Clement 8, 2.

as the performer of liturgy in the New Testament, the liturgist of the true holy place and the true tabernacle, which the Lord and no man fashioned. Here we recognize clearly that the primaeval mystery of the New Alliance is no liturgy in the usual, ritual sense; the expressions about the liturgy of the old covenant are being used in a higher sense concerning the purely spiritual facts of the new. Christ's sacrifice is not a liturgy in the old, ritual sense, but plain and noble reality, the ultimate and greatest fulfilment of what the old covenant had given in type. But when the church carries out the mystery of Christ in her own mystery of worship, in ritual, forms and expressions of the old covenant find a new and higher kind of reality, and fulfilment in the new rites. Here a liturgy arises which is first of all an exterior form, but does not carry 'a foreshadowing of good things to come';[1] rather it is the grace-filled reality, the redemption itself.

When we place the words 'mystery' and 'liturgy' side by side, and take mystery as mystery of worship, they will mean the same thing considered from two different points of view. *Mystery* means the heart of the action, that is to say, the redeeming work of the risen Lord, through the sacred actions he has appointed: liturgy, corresponding to its original sense of 'people's work', 'service', means rather the action of the church in conjunction with this saving action of Christ's. We saw above, that Christ and the church work together inseparably in the mystery; but we can none the less characterize mystery as more the act of the bridegroom, and liturgy the act of the bride, without thereby making too great a division. For when the church performs her exterior rites, Christ is inwardly at work in them; thus what the church does is truly mystery. Yet it is still proper to use the term liturgy in a special fashion for the church's ritual action. And this gives rise to the question, how has the mystery of the new covenant become liturgy?

The deepest ground for it lies in the fact we have already mentioned, that Christ has given the mysteries to his church. The Council of Trent teaches (Session XXII) that the new high priest, Jesus Christ 'was to offer himself to God once and for all on the altar of the cross, and there to accomplish everlasting salvation. But since priesthood was not to be extinguished through his death he left to his beloved bride, the church, a visible sacrifice, as human nature requires. Through it that bloody, unique sacrifice completed on the cross, was to be made present,

[1]Heb. 10, 1.

to continue the memorial of him until the end of time, and to apply his saving power to the remission of the sins we commit daily. After he had celebrated the ancient passover, which the multitudes of the sons of Israel sacrificed for a memorial of their coming out of Egypt, he instituted the new pasch for us, the slaughter of himself, handed on through the church by means of her priests, through visible signs, in memory of his passage from this world to the Father.'

The content, and so the essential form of the mysteries have been instituted and commanded by our Lord himself; he has entrusted their performance to the church, but not laid down to the last detail what is necessary or desirable for a communal celebration. By leaving the Spirit to his church, he has given her the ability as well, to mint inexhaustible treasure from the mystery entrusted to her, to develop it and to display it to her children in ever new words and gestures. Her bridegroom's love moves her to make of his gifts a praise to his love; her motherly goodness leads her to explain it to her children with all care, so that they may make it their own. So the liturgy, born of her fullness of the Spirit, and love, becomes a work of beauty and of wisdom.

It would be worthwhile to make clear this development of mystery into liturgy, with examples. But we must be content to point out some of the main lines of development. The Lord demanded a rebirth for entry into his kingdom; the natural man cannot reach God unless he first be changed. The old man must die, the new man, begotten out of God, must rise. 'If a man be not begotten of water and *pneuma*, he cannot enter heaven.'[1] *Pneuma* is the breath of God, from which supernatural life flows; it is God himself,[2] and his life dwelling in the new man. This word shows clearly that it is not a change of will that makes the Christian, but a completely new being, a 'sharing in God's being'[3] as St Peter says: we are then in the pure realm of grace and the invisible life of God. But the Lord says that the new man must be born again of water; thus the mystery of worship arises; for in the realm of God's supernatural action this birth from water can only be the exterior and visible expression of the inward, real birth from *pneuma*. It has therefore no natural worth of its own, but only symbolic value; this symbolic value is what the Lord says is absolutely necessary. For without this exterior act we could not recognize God's act. The plain, objective, sensible, tangible act of plunging into water is the pledge for the reality of God's new begetting; at the same time the community gives the

[1]Jn. 3, 5.   [2]Jn. 4, 24.   [3]II Peter 1, 4.

necessary witness that a new member has been added to it. It would be an error to think that it was enough to have a dumb dipping into water to form a picture of God's grace: water, matter from below, has no capacity for that. It must be complemented by something higher, formed and fashioned by it: the Spirit which comes from above. But what is better suited to express Spirit than the lightness and refinement of the Word, as the Lord speaks of it in the third chapter of St John's gospel? It gives motion to what thought would express; the ancients called it *Logos*, spirit-shaped, and thence it was so connected with *pneuma* that the two words are often interchanged. The element of sense and tangibility which the word indicated is clear. The fullness of the mystery comes from both: 'take away the word, and what is water except mere water. Word comes to the water, and the *mysterium* is there, itself like a word to be seen. Where does water have so great a power that when it touches the body, it should wash the heart? All of that from the mere word.'[1] The Lord called for a rebirth: the death of the old man. He himself showed us how it was to be done by dying on the cross and rising for God. Christians must be plunged into this death and resurrection, so that Christ's life, the life of the Trinity, revealed through him in the new alliance, might dwell in them. Therefore the candidate is stripped bare, as God made the first man, and as the second Adam hung on the cross.[2] The old man is to die and a wholly new one come out of the waters. The name of the Trinity is spoken over him; according to ancient Christian faith this meant that the whole power of the present Godhead came down upon this man and fashioned him anew by grace to God's own likeness. This plunging into Christ's death, and resurrection with him to God's life, as the words of Christ in St John's gospel (Chapter 2) describe it, is approved by St Paul as the meaning of baptism in his deep discourse in Romans (6). An extraordinarily rich store of meaning is contained in the simple words which St Matthew uses to tell of baptismal institution: 'go out, then, and teach all peoples to be disciples, baptising them in the name of the Father and the Son and the Holy Spirit, teaching them to observe all things which I have entrusted to you.'[3] How simply

---

[1] St Augustine *Tractatus in Joann*, 80, 3 cf 15, 4. The translation 'Word' does not give the full sense of λόγος; in later times this sentence of Augustine's was misused to make the sacrament a mere kind of sermon. This would have been impossible if there had been a proper understanding of λόγος—*verbum*.

[2] Cyril of Jerusalem, *Mystagogical Catechesis* II, 2.

[3] Mt. 28, 19.

this command is to be carried out is related in the story of the chamberlain's baptism by Philip.[1] They came to water, and the eunuch said, 'what is to keep me from baptism?' Both go into the water, the eunuch is put under, and made a Christian. Here we see the mystery in its simplest form, as it had to be under the circumstances.

With deep understanding and love the church has gradually expanded this simple rite and formed it into a rich service, without neglecting the mystery-centre. All the variety of texts, rites, and objects only serve to express the one content and do God honour, to bring it as close as possible to all the faithful. The candidate comes to the church; he is taken through repeated instruction in faith, which is the door to this new life; the blessed salt, wisdom's symbol, is given him; again and again the hand of the priest is laid on to bless him; exorcism is pronounced to drive out the evil enemy, and break the power of the demon over him; the secrets of the Christian way, the Our Father and the Creed, are given to him, yet only orally; written they might come to profane hands. He first hears nothing of the mysteries proper, baptism and eucharist, because he is not yet initiated, and as yet has no capacity to understand such things. We see how the church prepares and expresses ever more clearly the one side of baptism, the death of the old man, fallen to demons, and on the other gradually leads him into the region of holiness. Shortly before baptism the candidate has to repeat what he has learnt before the bishop: once more he is solemnly exorcised to make room for the coming of the Holy Spirit. Then comes the vigil. Out of the darkness of error, and of demons, out of the womb of life the divine light streams, and the new life in the Spirit is born. With a good teacher's insight, the church leads her children through the rites into their new life, of which they knew nothing before, shows them wonders of which they had only seen the shadows. The impression made on these men was all the more tense from waiting.[2]

First of all the radical turning away from the life they had lived before in paganism, found gripping and vivid symbolic expression in renouncing the devil, his pomps and his works. Candidates held out their arms to the West, towards the kingdom of darkness, blew, and with a sign renounced the devil eternally. Then they turned to the East, to the holy light and life, to Christ, the dawning from on high,[3] promised everlasting faithfulness to him, confessed him their master and acknowledged faith in him. Then they were stripped; nothing of human

---

[1]Acts 8, 26.   [2]Ambrose *De Mysteriis* I, 2.   [3]Lk. 1, 78.

making was to go with them down into the water; no work of man's mind: a wholly new man was to emerge. Then the whole body was anointed; this was a sign that the divine Spirit was to give them strength in the fight against the devil. Then they went down the three steps into the baptismal well; the water had been made holy beforehand by the bishop's *epiclesis*, invocation of the *pneuma*, and made fruitful for the new life, an image of the church's sacred womb. Three times they were plunged beneath the waters, and the name of the Holy Trinity called down upon them again; now the Trinity came and possessed them, sealed them with its own seal. From this point the positive aspect of the new life came out more and more.

Plunged under three times, the candidate came out on the other side of the well, three steps up; now, as initiate and new-born son, he was clothed in the white garment of light and immortality, and a burning light placed in his hands. He comes before the bishop who lays hands upon him, anoints him with the fullness of the god-life, first given in the waters. The new man, streaming with God's own light and glowing with love of him, goes up to the church where the baptised receive him with a kiss, and pray with him in fellowship for the first time. Now he may take part in the Eucharist, eat of the divine food and drink the blood of Christ which has become life for him. Milk and honey are given to him, the new-begotten child of God, who has entered the promised land and there sings songs of praise to the Lord. He is fully initiated, a fellow-subject with the saints and sharer of God's house, a member of Christ, a beloved son in the likeness of God's own Son; he awaits everlasting life.

Our brief description gives only a weak image of the rich liturgy which has grown out of the mystery of baptism. The sources, too, from which the church drew when she made the liturgy cannot be given here in detail, indeed can hardly be mentioned. Therefore we shall say a few words about them. The proper content of the mystery is given by the actions and words which the Lord has himself laid down. Still, he did not intend to create something completely new, to teach or fashion a new salvation. He used the age-old forms mankind had always known, changing them and improving them. The idea and even the form of some kind of baptism is a live thing among most of mankind, when purification from sin and passage into a new and holier life is to be expressed and realized. In particular the exterior rites and the objects used, because they are bound up with the natural movements of life and the things nature makes, are already, to a high degree, settled; water is water, whether it is used for natural rites of cleansing or highly elaborate rituals. The word is freer and more mobile; but it, too, is bound up with a language as it has grown to be. For his revelation God uses the word of human speech; it is thus that men are to understand him. The liturgy, too, uses human expressions and human formulae to make the mystery of God known. For the texts of its celebrations there is an extraordinary pattern in the Word of God in Scripture; here the Holy Spirit itself proclaims the gospel in the tongues of men, but with the power of God. Much is passed unchanged from the scripture into the liturgy, taking on a new form, a new dimension; from mere writing it has gone back to its first life.[1] In one special way this is true of the Old Testament word which receives a last light and a great richness in the liturgy of Christ's mystery. When, on Christmas night we read from Isaias, we read what is no longer prophecy but present fact. Here is the deepest ground for the allegorical or spiritual interpretation of scripture: since Christ appeared, we have the key to the Old Testament, the key which opens all doors: now we see not only the letter which kills, but the Spirit that gives life.[2] Nowhere have we a clearer recognition of the Spiral character of scripture than in the liturgy, where all its words are turned to praise of the mystery of Christ, or the life of the Christian in Christ.[3] The scriptural word is, as it were, born again from the heart of the church, and receives a new dimension; it becomes the voice of Christ crying out through the prophets and the church's voice, too. God's word has this about it, that unlike man's words it does not rise with the moment and disappear; it descends over and over again into the souls of God's people in the church, and while it continues there, it grows up again new, fresh and youthful. It comes to man begotten of the Spirit of God. The accusation so often heard, that you cannot pray spontaneously from the heart in age-old formulae, does not apply; this word rises spontaneously from the heart of the church our Mother.

---

[1] Cf Ildefons Herwegen in *Lit. Ztschrift* 3 (1930–31), p. 8 ff.

[2] II Cor. 3, 6; cf 14 f 'Until this day this veil remains with the Jews at the reading of the Old Testament. There must be a turning to the Lord first and then the veil will be taken away. . . .' This is true of the reading of the Old Testament in general, and the solution of all the difficulties brought against such reading.

[3] Cf Nicetas of Remesiana *De Utilitate Hymnorum* C.6 (In Psalmis) *Christi sacramenta canuntur*. All the mysteries of Christ from the incarnation to the second coming are mirrored in the Psalms.

The ceremonies of the law were unfit for use in the Christian liturgy in Christ's sacrifice; they had been fulfilled, and thus brought to an end. We should note that the Lord held his supper in connexion with the paschal meal, but that from the rite proper of the Jewish passover nothing went into the Christian eucharist; the ordinary table prayers were the first foundation of the Christian 'thanksgiving'.[1] Similarly, Christian baptism cannot be traced to the Jewish baptism of proselytes, although it has certain parallels with general human customs, from which that ceremony grew up as well.[2] In general we can take it that the Christian religion, as the fulfilment of all mankind's longing in the religious sphere, as the *catholic*, the common religion of mankind, takes to itself as of sovereign right and with sovereign freedom all that mankind has developed in truly great religious forms. If the Church were to shut herself off in fear from the world about her, she would not be the catholic church, but a sect. But she has accepted everything she found, into the world of her thinking, and thereby transformed everything; in her furnace she has cleansed everything from what was all too human, and left only the gold behind.

The 'plenitude of time'[3] when Christianity came into the world was peculiarly well-suited to give form to the liturgy. It was the mark of the entire ancient world that it had shaped the indwelling symbolism of the natural world into an elaborate yet simple language; this was particularly true of religious forms, and the mysteries we have just been speaking of. It was a custom in antiquity to anoint oneself after a bath with fragrant oil, for strength and beauty. The church has made this custom a rite of the new life by anointing the baptised, for an image of the sweet odour of the Spirit. Another custom was for a new-born child to take milk, mixed with honey. In many mysteries the 'new-born' received a cup of sweet milk: in just the same way, the Christians give their newly-begotten in Christ a drink of milk and honey; St Peter tells the young Christians, that like new-born children, they are to feel longing for the Spirit's milk, so they may grow in salvation.[4] It was similar with clothing. In the Greco-Roman world, clothing was not a casual or indifferent matter; with a new garment went a new manhood. In the mysteries a garment or a sign of the God was put on, and the

[1] Cf Strack-Billerbeck IV, p. 627 ff.
[2] Cf J. Leipoldt *Die Christliche Taufe im Lichte der Religionsgeschichte* (1928) and, on this book, J.L.W. 9, 203 ff.
[3] Gal. 4, 4. Eph. 1, 10.
[4] I Peter 2, 2.

initiate became that god. In connexion with these customs, Paul cries out, 'all of you who have been baptised in Christ, have put on Christ';[1] in Easter week the church sings this of the baptised who stand about the altar in their white clothing. This last example shows us once more that some customs which signify a mystical uniting with the godhead, were particularly well-appointed to serve the Christ-mysticism of the liturgy. Thus the age-old idea of representing the embodiment of divine strength with food and drink is brought up to its highest pitch of reality by the eucharist: a real meal with God, representing our deepest union with the god-man and rendering it fact, as the Lord himself says of it in John 6.

In these ways the whole of mankind, the whole creation has 'done service to the mysteries' as the blessing of water in the Roman Ritual says of it.[2] Similarly different elements make their own contributions, as do different peoples, races, and ages. Christendom, then, is Catholic, common to mankind; despite all unity in faith and moral teaching, it can and must express itself in a variety of ways. The liturgical forms of the sober, serious, lapidary Roman is one thing; the mystical depth and warmth of the orientals, the agile-minded, poetical Gauls, the dreamy and passionate Celts, or the cloudy, emotional Germans quite other things—to name only a few currents. Every people has expressed its pecularities in the liturgy, and made of them a sacrifice to God.[3]

But even within the one church different conditions have taken changing roles in the development of the liturgy. The clergy's part was a leading one, but laymen, too, have contributed with poetry, music, and the other arts; the liturgy of the seculars was not that of the monks, and the liturgy of cathedrals not that of village churches.

The whole church, therefore, and all conditions of men in her have worked together, and shaped the liturgical ornaments of the mystery, each man in his way, each according to his *charisma*, all on the ground of their inner sharing in the mysteries. The whole church is its bearer, as the Council of Trent says when it declares, 'Christ left behind the priesthood to his beloved spouse the church, so that by their service the church might carry out the mystical death'. Within her structure, every member acts his role in his appointed place, conjointed to all the rest; this is what Clement of Rome says. The God-appointed,

---

[1]Gal. 3, 27.
[2]*Creatura tua mysteriis tuis serviens.*
[3]A. Baumstark, *The Growth of the Liturgy* (Mowbray) 1957.

consecrated hierarchy holds the immediate and authoritative place of Christ as the actor of the mystery and high priest; the rest of the faithful, each according to his rank, form part of the church as Christ's bride. From thence it comes that the whole church, not merely the clergy is to take an active part in the liturgy, each according to sacred order, in his proper rank, place, and measure. All members are truly, sacramentally conjoined to Christ their head; every believer, because of the sacramental character he received in baptism and confirmation, has part in the priesthood of Christ the head. This means that the layman does not merely assist with private devotion and prayer at the priest's liturgy, but is, by his objective membership in Christ's body, a necessary and real sharer in the liturgical fellowship. It belongs to the perfection of this participation, of course, that this objective priesthood should be made real and brought up to its highest pitch by a personal sharing of life. As psychology teaches us, the inner life grows stronger to the extent that the external act corresponding to an interior one is consciously made: we hear a song, but the inner participation in it will be greatly heightened and made easier if we sing it ourselves. So with the liturgy, the decisive thing is inward participation which does not require unconditionally to be made external; but external participation does belong to the intense sharing of the experience, and to the completion of its symbolic expression.

In this, we must hold to the fundamental laws of the mystical body, as we have stated them: every member in its place, according to its duty and the measure of its grace. Laymen can never assume the service of the consecrated priesthood; every rank must keep its place. Everything is not for everyone, and not everything is immediately open to all. The mystery remains a mystery, and shows itself gradually to the eyes of the pure and the humble. So there is no esoteric cult of the liturgy, no aesthetic sampling; humility and purity of heart and openness to Christ, disclose the way to Christian mysteries. The meaning of the mystery is in a high degree something which belongs to ordinary people, precisely because they love the whole, and at the same time recognize that the things of God are hidden. But, as the fathers teach us, there are steps in knowledge; the outward expression of this is the reservation of sanctuary for priests, the choir for monks and virgins, and the people. Many of the difficulties of the liturgical renewal would disappear with a careful observance of the ancient notion of hierarchy. Is it not wisdom on the church's part to have put the *veil* of a ritual language over the liturgy, precisely because the mystery is not to stand in the fierce light of every day? Is it necessary to turn all texts into the vernacular, make every detail of every rite visible? Does not this take away something irreplaceable, the glow of veneration which means more to the people than understanding every detail? The obviously praise-worthy intention of bringing people back to active participation in the liturgy should not fall into the democratic heresy.[1] Hierarchy, that is to say, holy order and graduation of value must be maintained in the liturgy; in this way the true common life of the whole ecclesia arises; every order shares what belongs to it with the other. Common life does not mean everyone having the same, but each giving from his riches to the other to fill up that other's lack. Love is founded on mutual giving, and St Paul's word is fulfilled: by the mutual bond of aid in the strength of each member, the growth of the body is brought to fullness; the body is built up in God's love, *agape*.[2]

The sacred mystery is the visible expression, and at the same time the highest living activity of the mystical body of Christ: head and members are one in the sacrifice to the Father, to whom all honour goes up through the Son in the Holy Spirit, and from whom all grace and blessing come down through the same Word and Spirit. So ever deeper knowledge, and live sharing in the mystery become the central Christian theme of the sacrifice to God which pleases him, as Gregory of Nazianzen tells us in the Easter sermon:[3]

'We would bring a gift to him who suffered for us and rose. You might imagine I was thinking of gold or silver or precious fabric or stones; but all of this is passing earthly matter of which evil men usually have the greatest amount; no, we will bring ourselves as a gift, the thing most precious and most proper to God. We would give back the copy to its original, recognise what we are, give honour to our type, penetrate the meaning of the mystery, the reason of Christ's dying. Let each of us give all, give away all to him who gave himself up for us as the price of our freedom, for him who took our place. No one can give something greater than when, knowing the mystery, he gives himself, and, for Christ's sake, becomes all that Christ became for ours.'

[1] L. Verwilst O.P. has called attention to this false motive: *De stand van den priester aan het Altar* (Lit Tijdschr 11, p. 321–327), directed first of all against the attempt to place the altar in the middle of a church and thus remove a proper sanctuary. Verwilst sees this as a result of the levelling spirit, whereas the church has always striven to protect holy things for the sake of reverence.
[2] Eph. 4, 16.   [3] *Oratio I in Pascha*, P.G. 35, 397 ff.

3

THE ANCIENT WORLD AND THE
CHRISTIAN MYSTERIES

IT is a disheartening fact, that the wave of mysticism which is now passing over our age after the high tide of rationalism neither moves toward nor is in any way formed by the norms of Catholic Christendom. For the greatest part it loses itself in every kind of shallow bog and muddy pool, or foams away its power uselessly. This is not the fault of Christianity. On the contrary the religion of the *Logos* whose Spirit acts in the church and his appearance as a man among men, can show the only sure way and clear end to this longing. But Christianity, particularly in the centuries since the Renaissance and the Reformation has been looked upon so much as a mere juridical institution, a moral activity, a function of popular education, that the highest and finest desires and capacities of the human mind have only too often sought satisfaction elsewhere. At the very least mysticism became a special compartment in religious life, open only to a few, and by means of a special method. If today authority has to give warnings about occultism, theosophy, the 'Russian soul', and Oriental thought generally, it looks with high regard upon the German, Spanish and French mysticism of the late Middle Ages and the Counter-reformation. Yet it might be more suggestive to turn attention to that mysticism which blooms in the heart of the church herself, which belonged to her very being from the first, and which is therefore open to all Christians. It grows out of the common life, and gives the individual full satisfaction; Christ himself made it the way without which no one comes to the Father. It is therefore essentially Christian, essentially of the Church. We mean liturgical mysticism, the mysticism of the ordinary worship of the church, carried out and regulated by its priests; a mysticism, therefore, of sacred action, Spirit-informed, the property of the congregation led by proper authority, where the Lord himself shares its work with his bride and leads her to the eternal Father.

If we ask why this pure Christian ritual and congregational mysticism receded, the final answer will be found without any great difficulty in the modern decline of awareness of the God-given, objective mould which dominated the ancient world and the early middle ages. The theocentric attitude of mind was exercised, at least in shadowy form, in the ancient world by the humble subjection to nature, which was of divine fashioning; some enlightened minds, with Plato as their head, developed this view of nature and taught it. In Christianity the theme was brought to its splendid climax in the utterance: God is *agape*. This humble and therefore exalted attitude was broken, by another fall as it were, the self-emancipation of the age of Gothic and the Renaissance. In the latter period this revolution led to a self-divinizing heathendom. In their Reformation, the Germans, who, as St Clement Hofbauer said 'wanted to stay pious', produced a movement of personal piety, but destroyed consciousness of God as mystery. The first thing Luther rejected was the Canon of the Mass, containing the eucharistic sacramental mystery; he kept the communion, 'the Supper', as an expression of faith. In Catholic Christianity the mystery was kept in fact and protected by prescription; but it lost altogether too much ground in the piety of the people, giving place to the more subjective devotions which appeared, partly left over from the Gothic age, partly new creations.*

What the Christian of the ancient world brought with him from his old way of life, he had only to deepen and make more spiritual; he had a sense for objective norms and ideas, such as the modern man has to learn with effort and to make his own. Of course grace can take up the empty space, and compensate for what nature lacks; but in general the rule is true *gratia supponit et perficit naturam*: grace builds on and perfects nature.

From this point of view classical education which, because it was so bound up with nineteenth-century Liberalism and is therefore threatened by the latter's decline, takes on a new meaning for our future. It ought not to give merely formal and logical schooling; ancient form grows out of its own kind of consciousness. It is this consciousness which is a matter of life and death for our time more than any other. 'The powers which God sent to form the Christian thing made their entrance into history in the mighty framework of ancient culture, and in the works of the church fathers the well-springs of European culture brought to ripeness their most precious fruit.'[1] These 'powers which God sent' could develop even more intensively today if men's

[1] Proposition I of the Regensburg Diocesan Synod, 1927.

spontaneous ways of thought were better oriented towards the ancient ideal of an objective order of things which places the whole man, not just reason or emotion, into the cosmos of relations to God, his author and his end; and this is true not least for the life of piety.

When we consider ancient piety, we are struck by its strong sense for norms, its bonds to firm, traditional forms which lead to its expression in an objective, peaceful clarity and in communal action; we notice this even in apparently detached individual phenomena of a mystical type, which burst out of all firm and definite shapes. These characteristics are in no way true of more recent mystical life; their concepts have arisen from observation of more recent phenomena. This mysticism, rooted in the Orient and developed in most recent times by the Germanic peoples after the emancipation of the individual, is fundamentally different from ancient, formal, communal mysticism which gave shape particularly to the hellenistic mysteries, and then found its crown in Christianity.* The one sought a lone road, of purification and concentration, flying from the world, practising ascesis, turning aside from the common life: this was its way to God, its way into the godhead. The other acted in concert with God, as he graciously revealed himself, appeared on earth, and shared his saving act, his suffering, and new life with the initiate. The follower becomes one with the cult god of the fellowship, and with all its members, yet does not pass the boundaries of creaturehood. The origin of this mysticism is with God, not with merely human longing; it is bound up with authoritative form; the community gives it assurance, independent of its receiver, orderliness and rest, greatness which passes beyond the lone individual. Not merely upward-striving *eros* for the divine but Christian *agape* (the *caritas* of the Western fathers) which comes from above and gives itself in graciousness, holds and penetrates everything from the divine centre; it develops in humble self-giving to God and the brethren. From it alone a common life can grow: not from the striving of equal men, but from a principle which stands above all them, and preserves for personality its special worth.

Let us now consider this ideal vision of the whole in some detail, and the ancient mystery first of all. Of course it is not possible at this point to give a full treatment of even one of the mysteries; we must be content to show the main features of the ritual-type mysterium. In this we are on firm ground as well, since the discipline of silence has only left us a few unclear ideas about details. A relatively detailed description of an ancient initiation is to be had in the eleventh book of Apuleius' *Metamorphoses*. The author does, of course, omit the secret portion of the initiation proper, but he brings us extraordinarily well into the mood of the mystery religions and their piety in late antiquity. If we do not have exact information about any one mystery, we have a very clear concept from various reports of what the mystery was, especially the hellenistic mystery, in which Greek form joins an oriental other-worldliness. Whereas prayer would bring the thoughts and wishes of the mind before God, and sacrifice is essentially a gift to the gods, the mystery seeks to place itself in a still deeper relationship to them. The *Kyrios* of a mystery is a God who has entered into human misery and struggle, has made his appearance on earth (epiphany) and fought here, suffered, even been defeated; the whole sorrow of mankind in pain is brought together in a mourning for the god who must die. But then in some way comes a return to life through which the God's companions, indeed the whole of nature revives and lives on. This was the way of pious faith and sacred teaching (ἱερός λόγος), of society in the earliest mythical age. But the world, society is always in need of life; so the epiphany goes on and on in worship; the saving, healing act of God is performed over and over. Worship is the means of making it real once more, and thus of breaking through to the spring of salvation. The members of the cult present again in a ritual, symbolic fashion, that primeval act; in holy words and rites of priest and faithful the reality is there once more. The celebrant community is united in the deepest fashion with the Lord they worship; there is no deeper oneness than suffering and action shared. Thereby they win a share in the new life of God; they enter his chorus, they become gods. The mysteries' way is, therefore, the way of ritual action as a sharing in the gods' acts; its aim is union with godhead, share in his life.

The mystery, therefore, embraces in the first place the broad concept of ritual 'memorial'—ἀνάμνησις, commemoratio—the ritual performance and making present of some act of the god's, upon which rests the existence and life of a community. The sacred action becomes a mystery in the full sense when it is concerned not merely with strivings in this life, keeping the worshipping assembly in health and life, making nature blossom and thrive, but rather with union with the godhead which it honours and the blessed continuation of life after death as the centre of religious strivings. Ritual communities of this kind are brought together through the call of individuals with especially high aspirations; they form a class apart, close themselves off from the profane, and receive members by secret initiation. Their aim is σωτηρία, salvation, in the full fellowship of the god after death.

We can, then give a brief definition:

> The mystery is a sacred ritual action in which a saving deed is made present through the rite; the congregation, by performing the rite, take part in the saving act, and thereby win salvation.[1]

It is easy to recognize these characteristics, and the piety which belongs to them. In the first place the mystery is defined by a revelation (epiphany) from God; it is settled and prescribed by him; its piety is therefore theocentric. Next, the mystery is not concerned with race or nation, but with the individual, yet in such a fashion that this individual comes immediately into a community, under a religious authority. The act of separation from the profane, and the solemn initiation, give him a great insight into the new life; its mysticism finds practical application, not in purely individual, interior strivings, but in actions which all share; they lead to vision, not of a quietistic interior sort, but to the real showing of God. In them all the soul's faculties are engaged; the rite is sacred art of great stylistic value: rich drama, deep symbolism hold individual and congregation. It puts the individual into a gripping and upraising circle of divine action, carries him up beyond himself. In this kind of piety the danger associated with lonely prayer, of sinking down to self-contemplation, the possibility of outward sacrifices becoming mere show are easier to avoid.

I emphasize again that here I am only picturing the type. It will be asked in reply: where in antiquity will you find such a pure phenomenon? My answer to this is, we can nowhere exactly reconstruct the religious life of the ancient world; there was every degree of religious attitude; the ideal we have pictured above was nowhere fully realized. Yet that is so because in most cases ancient culture remained bound to the worship of nature, and the mystery rites often became purely animal rites, simply repulsive to a spiritually-minded man. But none

---

[1]E.g. my article 'Mystery-Piety' *Bonner Zeitschrift für Theologie und Seelsorge* (1926, 101–117) p. 104. Historical material is completed in J.L.W. 6, (1926) 113–204). See also Chapter II, ii above and the literature given there. For the relationship of *mysterium* to art and social history see Ildefons Herwegen, *Kirche und Seele* (1926); *Christliche Kunst und Mysterium* (1929) and the articles of A. L. Mayer in J.L.W. 5, 80–96; 6, 68–97; 8, 67–127; 10, 77–141; 14, 123–171; 15, 67–154. Finally Johannes Pinsk, *Germanentum und Katholische Kirche*: Abendland 2, (1926) p. 360–362 and 3, (1927–8) p. 17–19.

of that can prevent us from recognizing in the mystery a type of high
religious worth;[1] a worth, to be sure, which only received its full merit
in Christianity. St Paul says of the rites of the Old Testament, 'the
law held only the shadow of those blessings which were still to come,
not the full expression of their reality'.[2] How much more true that is of
antiquity. Yet an artist's first sketch is often of value to us in learning
more about his finished composition.

Yet before we pass over to the full picture, I want to give a summary
of the rich possible meanings which the word *mystery* had acquired in
the ancient world; it will serve to make its Christian use more intelligible.[3] Mysteries are originally the secret celebrations and consecrations
of the ancient mystery cults, the δρώμενα as a whole; next they are
the individual parts and elements of the mysteries: thus the sacred
λεγόμενα, the *symbola* and different formulas by which the initiates
recognized each other (sacred pass); then they are δεικνύμενα the things
shown, sacred objects in the *cista mystica*, symbolic and typical objects
which were shown at the high point in the visionary rite, the food of the
initiates, etc. All of these had holy dread about them and a fearsome
command of silence for their protection.[4] The mystically directed
philosophy uses the terminology of the mysteries to point up the
divinity, the hidden element in the theological δόγματα. Thus mysteries
especially in the visionary language of Plato, become the greatest and
deepest doctrine about godhead; godhead itself is the primeval
mystery, hiding itself in silence. When we speak of it at all we do so
in symbols which cover as much as they disclose. Heraclitus says, 'the
master at Delphi does not speak and does not conceal; he hints at
things.'[5] With this symbolic language for the things of God goes
allegory, not of the rationalist, Stoic kind, although it was happy to
lay claim to this splendid garment, but the mystical, platonist one. The
visible things of creation, the myths and sagas, the venerable rites
whose meaning is now often lost to us are treated as symbols of

---

[1]Only as a *type* can the ancient mystery point to the Christian mystery, which
reveals God's *agape*, since according to the myth a God is the Saviour of his
cult followers. In the realm of religious consciousness the mystery belongs more
to *eros*, the soul of the individual striving upwards to God. Cf Nygren, *Eros und
Agape* (1930) 140 ff.
[2]Heb. 10, 1.
[3]Cf *Theol. Revue* 24 (1925) 41–47: J.L.W. 8, 225–232.
[4]Vow to silence under oath has been found recently in a papyrus: Cumont,
Un fragment de rituel d'initiation aux mystères, Harvard Theol. Review 26 (1933)
151–160.*
[5]Diels Fr. 93.

theological wisdom. They point to the divine source which cannot be grasped or uttered in its wholeness. Theology becomes mystagogy, whose aim is to return to the primeval mystery. As such it remains ever connected in some way with worship, for it wills to be not simple abstraction, but the way to God. Theology and theurgy are part of the mystery.

The sober, practical religion of the Romans had neither concept nor word for mystery. It did possess a consecration to God, *devotio*, which was expressed particularly in oath-taking, above all the military one. This was called *sacramentum*. How easily an oath of this kind could be made into a kind of *mysterium*, a ritual obligation of the greatest force to the powers below is shown by Livy X, 38f, in his impressive picture of the oath recruits took in the 'Samnite legion' because of the flax about the place where they were sworn (*sacrata*). They were, as Livy says, initiated (*initiati*) according to the ancient rite of consecration (*ritu sacramenti*). The whole panoply of ritual was used; there were sacrifices and terrible oaths, so that the whole proceeding seemed more like initiation into a mystery than a military oath-taking; in particular he remarks on secret dedication (*occultum sacrum*) at the beginning, also of an oath of silence. This is clearly the beginning of the notion of *sacramentum* as consecration, mystery. This is even clearer in the report of Livy on the suppression of the cult of Bacchus by the Roman state in the year 186, when the consul in his accusation associates mysteries and military oath closely in the common term *sacramentum*: 'Do you imagine, citizens, that the young men who have been initiated with this rite (*hoc sacramento initiatos*) can be made soldiers?'[1]; how can the man who has been initiated take the sacred oath to the state? On the other hand Apuleius speaks of the military oath (*sacramentum*) which the *mystes* takes in the service of his God.[2] One sees the way which brought the word *sacramentum* into the terminology of the religious mysteries, a way full of meaning for Christian theology. Christians, even in the oldest translation of the Scripture, used the word *sacramentum* where μυστήριον could not be translated. So *sacramentum* took on the whole range of meaning μυστήριον had had. The whole ancient terminology passed into Christian usage, but in keeping with the higher spiritual level of the new religion it was made the bearer of higher and more

---

[1]Livy, Book XXXIX 15, 13; cf Reitzenstein, *Die hellenistische Mysterienreligionen* ed. 3 (1927) p. 192.
[2]Metamorphoses XI, 15.

spiritual concepts. The spiritualising process did not, however, lead to an evaporation of content; the word remained concrete, and kept its constant relationship to worship. The modern translation 'secret' in no way yields the deep, rich, concrete sense of the ancient word, but only on one side, mystic hiddenness, and this insufficiently. We recognize this immediately when we consider mystery in its Christian context, if only briefly.[1]

The last and supreme mystery of Christianity, the foundation and ultimate source of all Christian mysteries is the revelation of God in the incarnate *Logos*. God, who was hidden in timeless silence, advances into the world by a wonderful epiphany, showing himself in order to save mankind. This mystery is, therefore, an act, but an act which flows from God's depths and is therefore an endless plenitude of being. God 'made known to us the mystery of his will, according to the decision he took in Christ for the saving design in the fullness of the ages to sum up all things in Christ'.[2] St Paul has the task 'to illumine everyone as to what the design is of the mystery revealed from all ages in God, the creator of all things, so that the manifold wisdom of God may be made known to the principalities and powers through the church, according to the counsel of the ages which he took in Christ Jesus our Lord. . . .'[3] Here we see the Church brought into the mystery. St Paul praised God, 'who has power to set your feet firmly in the path of that gospel which I preach, when I herald Jesus Christ, a gospel which reveals the mystery, hidden from us through countless ages, but now made plain, through what the prophets have written; now published at God's eternal command, to all the nations so as to win the homage of their faith'.[4] John, without using the word mystery says the same thing: 'the Logos was made flesh and pitched his tent among us, and we had sight of his glory, glory such as belongs to the Father's only-begotten Son, full of grace and truth. . . . No one ever saw God; but now his only-begotten Son has himself become our interpreter.'[5] 'Life dawned; and it as eye-witnesses that we give you news of that life which ever abode with the Father and has dawned, now, on us.'[6] This everlasting life is Christ himself; therefore the epistle to the Colossians calls him the mystery: God's design to save is contained in the person of Jesus, and Christian being is: 'knowledge of the mystery of God, of Christ in whom are all

[1]Cf detailed presentation Ch II supra.
[2]Eph. 1, 9 ff.   [3]Ibid 3, 9 ff.   [4]Romans 16, 25 ff.
[5]Jn. 1, 14 and 18.   [6]I Jn. 1, 2.

the hidden treasures of wisdom and *Gnosis*'.[1] The epiphany of Jesus Christ in which godhood, manhood, heaven and earth, spirit and matter meet and unite, through which the holy Spirit came down to bring the world healing: this saving act of God is the real mystery for the Christian. 'The birth of Christ and the whole saving design, then, are one great sacrament, since in the visible man the divine majesty did that inwardly for our consecration which took place in a secret invisible fashion through its power. Therefore the incarnation is rightly called a mystery or sacrament.' Thus, in summary of patristic teaching, the monk of Corvey, Paschasius Radbert (860).[2] But the high-point of the whole saving drama is the death and crown of resurrection, when Christ entered the inmost heart of God in all his manhood, and found everlasting redemption. The pasch of the Lord, his death and exaltation is the mystery of redemption proper, the high-point of God's plan. The saved church comes out from it; the new covenant is built on it, the eternal covenant of Christ's blood. Upon it rests all salvation.

It is Christ's will that this spring should always be running in the church. Not just faith in the once dead prince is to save the faithful; his saving act is to be a continual, lasting, mystical and yet concrete presence in the church, from which the power of his blood is to flow daily to give life and healing to the faithful. The promise, 'I am with you all days until the end of the world'[3] is to be fulfilled not merely by the moral or spiritual protection of grace in abstract, but in a concrete yet Spirit-filled presence and objective nature. Therefore the Lord left behind him for his church not merely faith and Spirit but his mysteries; or rather, he ordained that the life of faith and grace should find continual new stimulus and expression in the church through the common celebration of the mysteries. The words of Christ, 'where two or three are gathered together in my name I am in the midst of them' were to be quite literally fulfilled.[4]

For this reason the Lord instituted the mystery as the last act of his life in this age. On the evening of his betrayal, in expectation of his dreadful passion and in the confidence of the victory which his obedience to the Father would bring, he gave to his disciples this mystical celebration of his redeeming deed: *tradidit corporis et sanguinis sui mysteria*

---

[1]Col. 2, 2: εἰς ἐπίγνωχιν τοῦ μυστηρίου τοῦ θεοῦ, Χρίστου. The vulgate *in agnitionem mysterii Dei Patris et Christi Jesu* completely destroys the sense.
[2]*Liber de Corpore et Sanguine Dui*, ch. 3. Migne PL 120, 1275 ff.
[3]Mt. 28, 20.
[4]Mt. 18, 20.

celebranda.[1] The bread becomes his body, the chalice his blood; the body is offered in sacrifice, the blood flows as the sacrificial blood of the new covenant: clear, symbolic yet real presentation of the death of Christ. The mystical bread and the mystical wine are at once food and drink for life; yet life can only come out of that death which leads to resurrection. Even the invitation, 'do this in memory of me', shows that the Lord did not die for ever, but lives on. In the mystery marvellous things are joined: death and life, pain and blessedness, human sorrow, and the delight which only God knows. Through death to this age he leads the way to everlasting salvation and the riches of the age to come. This sacred rite with its full divine content is what the disciples are to 'act in memory'; they are to make real again the passion of their divine master. As the church grew out of the Lord's blood, she is to live and grow in his strength. Still in heaven with his Father, each day he wills to sacrifice himself with her fighting and suffering on earth, wills to celebrate his death with her in the world by a mystical and symbolic act, and so to waken her to a new life, in and with God. Christ has given his mystery to the church's care; she acts it out, and thereby fulfils his action, which has become hers. So Christ and the church become one in act and passion: the mystery is made a new and eternal covenant. The saving act continues and is crowned in the oneness of everlasting love, until the symbol comes to an end and only the pure reality shows itself to the seeking eye in eternity.

From the mystery of redemption flow the other mysteries as does all grace; the cross which overcame sin and death, gave everlasting life. First there is baptism, a mystical-real sharing in the Lord's death for this world of sin and his new life for God. It is completed and fulfilled by anointing with the new, supernatural principle of life, the *pneuma Christi*. By this every Christian becomes a true Χριστός, an anointed one, who now has a share in the spirit of God: θείας κοινωνοὶ φύσεως.[2] As Christ is by his nature Spirit ('the Lord is pneuma'[3]) and has revealed himself in glory since the resurrection, so, too, the Christian, risen in baptism, has a real share in the divine Spirit by grace. He carries the seal of Christ, the supernatural likening to the Lord through grace; the new life is nourished and strengthened in the Spirit by the eucharist, the Spirit's food. The Christian's initiation is carried out in these three

[1]Roman Canon on Holy Thursday: 'He gave the mystery of the body and blood to his disciples, for them to celebrate.'
[2]II Peter 1, 3.
[3]II Cor. 3, 17.

mysteries. Washing, anointing, and food bring him to his Christian's fulness. As a mature Christian, he can actively participate, taking his share in the offering, celebrating it with Christ. For all the anointed are a 'holy, royal, priesthood, appointed to make offering in the Spirit, to please God through Jesus Christ'.[1] How the mystery develops among the various conditions of life and situations, cannot be gone into here.[2] All the church's blessing and consecrations are a communication from the cross, or in liturgy, a redemptive grace proceeding from the mystery of the mass. St Leo the Great writes:[3] 'thy cross is the spring of all blessing, the cause of all graces. Through the cross power is given to him who believes in place of weakness, glory in place of shame, life in place of death. Now the variety of fleshly sacrifices is ended; all the many sacrificial gifts lead up to fulfilment in the one offering of thy body and blood. For thou art the true lamb of God, who puts out the world's sin; thou dost fulfil all mysteries. As there is now one sacrifice for all the sacrificial gifts, there is now only one kingdom, formed of all peoples.'

When Leo says the crucified Lord is the 'fulfiller of all mysteries', of the typical sacrifices and rites of the Old Testament, that is true in a sense of the ancient mysteries. They, too, as the fathers and St Augustine in particular say of the heathen sacrifices, were shadows, if misleading ones, of the true mystery to come. We can understand, then, that the fathers with advancing clarity discover the true mystery in Christianity and seek in some way to express divine truth by using the terminology of the mysteries, (purified and raised), for the Christian rites. Cyprian talks of *dominicae passionis et nostrae redemptionis sacramentum*:[4] the mystery of the Lord's passion, at the same time the mystery of our redemption. And there he merely summarizes clearly the meaning of what was taught before him. But from the 3rd century onwards this teaching is always clearer, expressed in greater detail and better formed in the liturgy; we have not space for more details here.[5]

And really what the ancient world longed for but only attained in so shadowy and imperfect a form is now fulfilled by Christ's coming in grace, fulfilled in an over-powering fashion; it is so wonderful that men

---

[1] I Peter 2, 5.
[2] Cf II, i above.
[3] Sermo VIII *de Passione Domini*, PL 54, 339 ff.
[4] Epistle 63, 14.
[5] A detailed collection of the most important texts in my *Das Mysteriengedächtnis der Messliturgie* J.L.W. 6, p. 113 ff and 13, p. 99 ff.*

can have had no inkling of it. This is the point where divine love and divine life come down upon the poor earth, take a share in the poverty of mankind, overcome sin which has once more brought chaos into the world, create the sacrificial deed to conquer worlds by the death of an incarnate God, restore the oneness of God and man, heal and glorify the creature. Out of the blood of the dying God-man and the glory of his transforming light (δόξα) eternal salvation flows, divine life for those who belong to him. All of this was at work in the new alliance, the *ecclesia*, in the vast simplicity of her Spirit-informed rites filled with symbolism and reality beyond the scope of worlds. In this form the noblest possession of mankind's religious strivings was concentrated, purified from animal and sordid elements, given shape in the school of Greek aesthetic teaching, the breath of oriental mysticism upon it, and ennobled by its service of God. Its content was totally new: the gift of divine grace: *de tuis donis ac datis*.[1]

The best of the ancient world did service to Christendom. The service was extremely desirable; in Christianity the mystery-type gained a wholly new meaning. The sacrificial service of the old alliance was done away with, or better, fulfilled with the sacrifice of Christ. With this came the new age: the old was past. In the Church of the new alliance there could only be one sacrifice, the sacrifice of Christ. If it was to act through the centuries, it could only do so by its mystical presence in the sacrament, *in mysterio*, in the worship of the Church which the new alliance had made. In the mystery, Christ lives in the Church, acts in her and with her, preserves and enlivens her. In the mystery we too already breathe the air of the coming age of God's Kingdom and have our conversation in humble faith. For the mystery is the mystery of faith; faith alone grasps the *virtus sacramenti*, the grace contained in the mystery. When faith passes over into vision, the veil of the mystery will fall and we shall see the godhead it contains.

The sacred rites belong to this veil. Antiquity shared in its creation, and so has deserved of Christ; without the form there would be no knowledge of its content. Thus, Hellenism wins a God-given meaning for the whole history of the world.

Clement of Alexandria, the great scholar and Hellenist, said that through the Logos the whole world had become Greek; he once compared the ancient mysteries with those of Christ (his first thoughts were on the spiritual vision, but the symbolic action in worship came in too).

[1]'Of thy gifts and presents', Roman Canon.

He saw in paganism only deep shadows, after which light rose which he greeted, full of happiness: χαῖρε νέον φῶς: welcome, new light![1] But those shadowy contours helped him in some way to express the new, inexpressible wonders:[2] 'O marvellous, holy, mysteries, O pure light. By torch-light I shall be brought to see heaven and God. I shall be made holy by the consecration. The Lord is heirophant: he brings the initiates to the light and puts his seal upon them. He presents the believers to the Father, that they may be kept for eternity. This is the thunder of my mysteries. When you wish, you may be initiated; then you will join the circle of angels which surrounds the unbegotten, unchanging, the only God; God's Logos will be our guide.'

[1]Firmicus Maternus, *De Errore profanum religionum*, 19, turns the mystery formula, 'hail, bridegroom, hail young light', on Christ: 'There is one light, one true bridegroom whose name Christ has kept.'

[2]*Protrepticus* 124, O. Stählin I, p. 84 cf there the whole passage which is clearly inspired by the *Bacchae* of Euripides.

4

THE CHURCH'S SACRED YEAR*

WITH every first Sunday of Advent we begin another church year. The cycle begins anew, and starts from the beginning. Is its only meaning didactic? Repetition, they say, is the mother of all learning. We have, perhaps, not drawn the value out of the old year sufficiently; does not the church therefore give us occasion to live through the whole once more? Of course this motive is present; the church knows how to teach. We are to go on celebrating the same events, so long as life lasts, exhausting the whole content of the church year and making it our own. What was neglected last year can be made up in this, the gaps filled in. And when we have lived all to its full we can still deepen what we have won and come to know. Like a path which goes round and up a mountain, slowly making the ascent to the height, we are to climb the same road at a higher level, and go on until we reach the end, Christ himself.

But didactic reasons alone cannot exhaust the meaning of return and cycle in the church's year. For we imperfect men are not properly its bearers: rather in it we join a higher sphere of action. The real actor in the church year is the mystical Christ, the glorified Lord Jesus, together with his bride the church, who in her inmost being is with him in heaven already. John has seen her: 'the holy city of New Jerusalem, come down from heaven and from God, ready like a bride adorned for her husband.'[1] St Paul in his letter to the Galatians calls her 'the Jerusalem above, the free woman who is our Mother'.[2] The fathers, therefore, speak of 'the church of heaven' (Tertullian for example, *On Baptism*, 15: *una ecclesia in caelis*.) And where else can the bride be except where her bridegroom is, at God's right hand? 'God has called us to life in company with Christ, raised us up and put us at his right hand in Jesus Christ.'[3] This *ecclesia*, bound up so intimately with her Lord does not celebrate the mystery in a negligent or half-awake fashion. She has his own strength and power; he is present in the fullness of these mysteries. The Church whose head towers into eternity, while

---

[1] Apoc. 21, 2.   [2] Gal. 4, 26.   [3] Eph. 2, 5 ff.

part of the body remains on earth—its still imperfect members—has no need of the continual change which is a characteristic of physical nature. Nature is always in flux, always changing: things rise and fall, are brought to birth and perish. But Christ and his church stand above nature, in the realm of abiding Spirit; they do not require continual flow and change; the phrase 'church-year' should not lead us to bring naturalistic notions into the realm of God.[1]

When, therefore, the church speaks of a 'year' or as the ancients did of a yearly cycle (*anni circulus*) it is in connexion with other ideas. The circle for the ancients is precisely the opposite of all development: as something completely round it is the symbol of eternity, of God. In the circle there is no before or after, no greater or less; it contains the highest point of likeness and oneness. The circle has neither beginning nor end. It returns upon itself and stretches out to all directions; it is the deepest rest and the highest exercise of power. The circle is, then, an image of life, but of life without development, without growth; of eternal life and fullness (πληρῶμα). Circle and sphere are the sensible images of eternal perfection. The sacred course of the liturgy is to speak of eternity not of nature, which comes, blooms, puts forth its fruit, then fades and dies. So there is no dying in the church year, only life, even in the way through death. Nature has a shadowy eternity in her capacity to come back to life after fading and sinking away; but death always comes again; how short the bloom is, how long the dying and the death. There is no winter in the church's year; if in spite of that, it starts up again, circle forming on circle this constant return is meant to suggest the divine quality of the mystery. St Ambrose in his morning hymn calls Christ, 'the true day which shines on day, the true Sun which casts everlasting splendour'. Christ is therefore the day which is splendid with the light that knows no evening, as the Greek liturgy says.[2] Christ is also the true year, whilst the world's day is the *aion*, or rather, Christ is the Lord of all the ages (αἴωνα).[3] This is so not because he perpetually renews himself, like natural light, but because

---

[1]This does not mean a rejection of natural symbolism which, on the contrary, has great meaning for the church. But it is to be noted that the earliest fathers see in the change of the seasons not an expression of natural life, but a symbol of resurrection. Therefore on tombs in the catacombs we often find the four seasons. The same picture had a completely different meaning in ancient painting.

[2]Φῶς ἀνέσπερον.

[3]Cf I Tim. 1, 17 where it is said of God: 'to the King of ages, immortal, invisible, only God: honour and glory in age of ages.'

he is light and life without winter, darkness or decline. Christ saves spirits; he is the saints' light in heaven; in the church year on earth he gives us a mystical reflection of his own everlasting day with God.

In heaven the glorified Lord is the very content of eternal life for all the saints; on earth his mystery is the spring of the church's life. They live seeing; we walk in faith. We do not see the Lord in glory but possess him already in faith and in the mysteries which he gave to the church on leaving her. The church year is therefore the mystery of Christ.

As the uninterrupted sun Christ shines in heaven; 'that city needs neither sun nor moon, because the glory of the Lord shines upon it and the Lamb is its brilliant light'[1] so the light of Christ shines upon us through the symbols of the mysteries. Therefore St Ambrose addresses Christ: 'I find thee in thy mysteries.'[2]

The mysteries of Christ, however, have a special two-sided character of their own. In themselves they are divine, supernatural, Spiritual; yet they mirror temporal action. We live the Lord's year in this world, have here experience of his birth, growth, maturity, suffering and death. His resurrection and upraising to the Father's right hand truly take us across into the kingdom of God. But the second coming, the last entrance of Christ into the world ($\pi\alpha\rho\text{ου}\sigma\text{ί}\alpha$) is an event in time; at that point the glorified Lord will show himself for the first and only time to the whole world; that will be the last moment of succession in time.

In any case the church year contains so much of the Lord's earthly life, that since the end of the late middle ages it has been taken as a spiritual participation and contemplation of that life.

Would this still be a mystery? It would be a moral sharing in the life and feeling of Jesus, but no mystical, oneness with Christ the Kyrios in the order of being, not the oneness which, according to his teaching and that of his apostles, is the aim and meaning of Christian life. We should not be plunged into his Spirit, into God's eternal life. If that life has its rôle in the church's year, then the year must have another meaning.

It is not that common life and consciousness with Christ are excluded; the church reads to us from the gospels for us to consider, weigh and imitate. But because she knows that our own thinking can never lead to the heart of God, that our prayer lacks wings to take it up unless it is carried by God's Spirit, she plunges all the moral meanings into this Spirit.

---

[1] Apoc. 21, 22   [2] *Apologia Prophetae David,* 58

Christ comes to us in two ways which are really only one. There is a Christ of history and a Christ of faith; but the two are one: it would be dangerous to regard only the one or the other. Jesus, a man living in time, could not redeem us; the Christ we see in the mysteries alone would move in a breathless air. Our redemption rests upon the fact that God has really appeared in the flesh and that this man is the Son of God and *Kyrios*, glorified at the Father's right hand. The Christ of history was born as a man, lived in Galilee and Judaea and the streets of Jerusalem, prayed and struggled on the Mount of Olives, died on Golgotha. The glorified Christ, in Spirit rose, awakened, and went up to the Father; thence he sends his own Spirit, dwells, an invisible powerful presence in the church and in every man who has faith, is baptized, and has love.

The man Jesus has risen up to a name above all names, through all of this: he was crushed in the flesh of sin, bore the form of a servant, was obedient to death; he became *Kyrios, pneuma.* He is, then, the same Lord who walked unnoticed and persecuted through the fields of Palestine and at last ended his time like a criminal on the cross; now he rules the world as King and the church is his bride. All his life, beginning in the Virgin's womb, is the great mystery of salvation, hidden from eternity in God and now revealed in the *ecclesia*. The deeds of his lowliness in that life on earth, his miserable death on Calvary appear now in a wholly different, light, God's own light; they are his acts, revealed, streaming with his light.

This life of the *Kyrios*, this great course from the Virgin's womb and the manger to the throne of his majesty on high, this mystery, is what we in the church share. The great facts of redemption are for us to celebrate and possess, not merely heartfelt considerations of our Lord's earthly life in all its details, and an imitation of it. A person without baptism could do that: a Christian and a Catholic celebrates the mystery of Christ.

And celebrate he does in a wholly concrete, immediate fashion, vast, divine. It is not thoughts of our own devising we are to think—how powerless we are before the acts of God—but thoughts to which the Spirit gives power; nor do they come in simple acts of illumination and special gifts of grace, but in the same Spirit's objective reality. The liturgical mysteries represent the saving acts of Christ to us, from incarnation to eternal rulership in living, concrete reality, yet in a manner telling of God their spiritual source: it is from the Saviour's own spring we drink. We who are not yet in glory, who still are in pain beneath the burden of sin, can go the way of redemption with the humbled Christ for company, die to sin. Christ has made his way present in the mystery, a saving way. Christ's phrase, 'I am the way'[1] is realised here in the deepest fashion. He does not merely point the way to us, he is the way; he carries us forward to the goal. His birth is now no longer an unimportant birth in Bethlehem, the idyll of the crib which so many took it for, but a serious event of poverty and lowliness, illumined, of course, with the light of divine love and greatness. The *mysterium* shows this birth as the burning appearance of God in flesh to redeem and heal the world, to unite heaven and earth. His death is now no longer the terrible, tortured dying on the horrid wood, a criminal's execution, but the sacrificial death of the god-man, the public service of the one high priest, the Son's devotedness in bringing the only sacrifice worthy of the Father, from which all life was to flow out on the sinful world: the spring of resurrection.

So the mystery reveals to us the real meaning of Christ's saving deeds in time. It takes none of the concreteness from them, but rather places them in their real, divine context, shows them to be a part of God's saving plan, hidden from eternity revealed now in time, and flowing back into eternity. 'Through the man Christ, to Christ, God.' This great theme of St Augustine takes shape in the mysteries: man is the way and God the end. History shows itself as the carrying out of God's design and its return into eternity.

When, therefore, the church year celebrates historical occurrences and developments, it does not do so for its own sake but for that of eternity hid within it. The great deed of God upon mankind, the redeeming work of Christ which wills to lead mankind out of the narrow bounds of time into the broad spaces of eternity, is its content.

Yet this content is not a gradual unfolding in the sense that the year of nature naturally develops: rather there is a single divine act which demands and finds gradual accustoming on men's part, though in itself complete. When the church year fashions and forms a kind of unfolding of the mystery of Christ, that does not mean it seeks to provide historical drama, but that it will aid man in his step by step approach to God, an approach first made in God's own revelation. It is the entire saving mystery which is before the eyes of the church and the Christian, more concretely on each occasion. We celebrate Advent, not by putting

[1] Jn. 14, 16.

ourselves back into the state of unredeemed mankind, but in the certainty of the Lord who has already appeared to us, for whom we must prepare our souls; the longing of ancient piety is our model and master. We do not celebrate Lent as if we had never been redeemed, but as having the stamp of the Cross upon us, and now only seeking to be better conformed to the death of Christ, so that the resurrection may be always more clearly shown upon us.

It is, therefore, always the glorified *Kyrios* whom we have in our spiritual vision, even when we call out, 'Thou who dost sit at the Father's right hand, have mercy upon us'. The whole church year is, therefore, a single mystery. Its high-point is mystery in the highest sense, the *sacramentum paschale*, the sacrificial mystery which is brought to us again each Sunday. There the redemption, which reaches its height in the sacrifice of the Cross and the glory of the church which goes from that resurrection, are mystically carried out and brought to the faithful. In the course of time this celebration of the paschal mystery has been extended from Septuagesima to Pentecost. Of course there is, especially in this season, a rich unfolding of the mystery for us to observe, one which in greatest part is connected with the historical acts of Jesus' life. But nonetheless it is not a sort of dramatisation of Christ's earthly life. This is clear since throughout it is the whole mystery which takes place in the mass; the mysterium is always whole.

Out of the paschal mystery, which in the first age of liturgy was the one ruling motif, there developed the epiphany, for which Advent (*adventus:* ἐπιφανεία) prepares us even today, although the Christmas feast has now been placed before it. The showing, epiphany, includes Christmas but is more than the feast of Christ's birth. Again, it is the entire redemptive mystery, seen under the view-point of the incarnation. When God takes flesh, he consecrates it. Is there, then, a proper mystery of the incarnation, as there is of Christ's death? No. We celebrate the culmination of epiphany, too, by the memorial of Christ's death: redemption was first finished upon the cross. Because the world lay in sin, it had first to be quit of this burden. Epiphany is, therefore, the entire mystery of redemption, seen from another vantage point: the Lord only became man, as the Scripture and the fathers teach us, in order to die on the cross, so to give back to the Father mankind which was dead through sin. 'When he came into the world he said, sacrifice and gifts thou wouldst not have; but a body hast thou readied for me. There was no good pleasure in thy eyes for burnt offerings.

Then I said, look, I come—thus it is written of me in the book—to do thy will.'[1]

The mystery of the church's year is one. Does not this emphasis on unity then take away the attractiveness of variety which never leaves the spirit weary but informs and stimulates it continually? No; unity does not mean uniformity. The more single an idea is, the deeper it is and the more powerfully it fills the mind: so the fullness of its conception seeks an outlet in a variety of rites. The mass is always the high-point of liturgy, because it contains the mystery of redemption in its source, the passion and resurrection of Jesus. But from the source a mighty stream of mysteries flows into the Church's ground, and on its banks the Spirit's Word forms ever new pictures in the liturgy, to clothe and express the rites. The words of Scripture and the liturgy are no mere human words, which arose in a merely human mind and pass on, like a breath of wind, without a trace. The Word of God is full of the power of God. 'As snow falls from heaven and rain as well, and returns not, but the earth drinks it down, and grows fruitful and green, so is it with my word which leaves my mouth: it comes not back to me empty. It carries out what I will, goes the way whither I send it.'[2] The Word takes part in the active power of the mysteries. 'Sacrament is also the divine writings where the Holy Spirit acts inwardly by the quickening word,' says Paschasius Radbert.[3] In the word, too, there is a divine presence. 'We would hear the gospel, the Lord present,'[4] says St Augustine, and this was the reason why the congregation stood at the reading of the gospel. 'The Abbot should read the gospel aloud while all stand in reverence,'[5] St Benedict writes. St Jerome is not afraid of putting the mystery of the Holy Scripture immediately after that of the eucharist: we eat his flesh and drink his blood not only in the mystery but in the reading of scripture.[6] In an old sermon for the Annunciation we read, 'the coming of our Lord and Saviour . . . is celebrated by the church in the whole world, and its yearly return brings it great joy; for what the world of believers once came to know when its salvation came, has hallowed the feast for the world which came after, throughout all generations. . . . Now, therefore, the miracle

---

[1]Heb. 10, 5–7; Ps. 39, 7–9.
[2]Is. 55, 10 f.
[3]*De Corpore et Sanguine Domini* 3, PL 120, 1276; cf J.L.W. 8, 207.
[4]*Tract. in Joan*, 30, 1.
[5]*Regula* Ch. 11.
[6]Cf passages in J.L.W. 8, 210 f.

of the past is put before our eyes when the godly readings tell us year by year of things past, and these are piously celebrated in yearly recurrence.'[1]

From this presence of the God-man's acts in *Logos* and *ritus* it becomes clear, too, how the church, although she always possesses the whole of the mystery of Christ, can still, on certain days when a definite aspect of it is brought into the light, sing, 'to-day': at Christmas, 'to-day Christ is born'; Epiphany, 'to-day the heavenly bridegroom is joined to the church'; Easter, 'this is the day the Lord has made'; Pentecost, 'to-day the *pneuma* appeared to the disciples in fire'. The entire holy year is an image of the eternal design of God, contains the mystery of Christ; within this circle the mystery unfolds to the Vision that cannot yet see the whole as it is in the world to come. As the entire year carries in it a divine presence, the individual day within this cycle takes up once more the saving event which once sanctified it.[2] While the visible symbols give expression, by their abiding sameness, to the mystery's oneness, the lighter, more mobile word can make present its variety and fullness. We celebrate mass each day as a whole redemptive mystery; yet, in the divine Word, it is the incarnation which is present at Christmas and Epiphany, the suffering and up-raising of Christ which is present to us at Easter. Always it is God present, not mere human reflections, which is the meaning of the mystery. How otherwise could St Benedict tell his monks, 'let us await the Pasch with the joy of the Spirit's longing.'[3] The mystery of worship is presence then, not in the bonds of time, but in the freedom of God and his Spirit.

When the man who has been knit into the church celebrates the mystical year with her, his mother, as a true mystery, all the truth it contains becomes his own; what Elizabeth said to Mary is fulfilled: 'blessed is she who has believed; for the things said to her by the Lord shall have their fulfilment.'[4]

---

[1]Perhaps by Proclus of Constantinople. Printed among the works of St Leo: PL 54, 580.
[2]Cf e.g. the hymn for Christmas: ' "This present day" (*hic* not *sic !* is the older reading) shows, as the cycle of the year returns, that thou hast come as the world's salvation.'
[3]Regula Ch. 49.
[4]Lk. 1, 45.

5

THE CHURCH'S SACRED DAY

As the year is an image of the life of man and of mankind and thus of sacred history, each day too, with its rising of light and life, its growth to zenith and descent to sleep, forms an image which can serve as framework and symbol of the mystery of Christ. As Christ's sacrificial death is the climax of the world's history, mass is the climax of the day. In the church's year the *Logos* explains and expands the paschal mystery; in a single day the office clothes and comments on the mass: the office is the prayer which the Church puts round about the sacrifice.

The highest acts of every religion are prayer and sacrifice. The more spiritual a religion, the higher and more spiritual its concept and vision of these things. The exterior material sacrifices of Jews and pagans had an external, ritual prayer: the more pure, deep and inward, the more spiritual this prayer, the higher the notion of sacrifice which will accompany it. The more man sought to approach God in prayer with a real submission of mind, the less that prayer was lip-service and external form; it became a real call to God from the soul's depths, or a conversation with him.[1] To the extent that this took place, the accompanying sacrifice became a full and selfless gift to God and the community. Thus prayer came more and more to correspond to its ideal, while on the other hand sacrifice, 'gift made to God', fulfilled its task of expressing the inner devotion of the will to God; the two drew near and were formed into one: sacrifice became, in a deeper sense than had been known before, the high-point of the life of prayer.

The spiritualising of the notion of sacrifice brought a danger with it. If the essence of sacrifice is the inward adherence to God, perhaps it would be better to do away with all external and exterior acts, and have only the pure devotion of the mind in prayer. This conclusion was drawn by many circles of pious pagans at the time Christianity was growing, in late antiquity, and by many Jews, too; all external, visible

---

[1]'Prayer is bold, a conversation with God,' Clement of Alexandria, *Stromata* VIII, 39, 6; cf also 42, 1, 49, 1.

worship was to fall away, or be confined to common prayer, which themselves could be just as well or better performed by the individual, recollected, undisturbed by the world about him. The danger came that the whole of worship would go inside man, that all religion would end as unbridled individualism and subjectivism, revolving round men rather than God.

In this as in everything else, Christianity gave its approval to all the excellence which the ages before Christ had discovered; still it remained infinitely superior to any non-Christian religion. It recognised of course that the external, material rites of pagan and Jewish ages were to be done away with in the new covenant. Now there was to be only a 'sacrifice in Spirit': an expression which is still preserved by the *oblatio rationabilis*, the λογική θυσία of the Oriental liturgy. Yet this spiritual sacrifice is equated with the sacrifice of the mass, that is, with an external, liturgical celebration carried out by priest and people in concert and bound up with the rite of bread and wine. In spite of that, there is nothing external or material mixed up in it. For behind the visible, objective action is a wholly spiritual reality: the person of Christ, the Word incarnate, who, under the veil of mystical figures, presents his loving act of devotion to the Father in dying. The community joins with his sacrifice, its self and consciousness filled with the Spirit of God, and inspired by it, and completes with him a wholly spiritual sacrifice to God. Objectivity and personal sharing are joined in a loving unity: objectivity is made spiritual and inward; subjectivity finds a firm and changeless hold on the divine action of Christ which raises a man's action to himself and first gives it power and meaning. The vine gives the sap of life to the shoots; in this strength they can bring out rich fruit.

The act of Christ in the Christian sacrifice consists in his presenting once more his act of sacrifice and redemption beneath the veil of symbols; the share of the faithful expresses itself in the co-sacrifice, especially in the prayer which surrounds the sacrifice; therefore the *eucharistia* plays so important a rôle in the mass, particularly in the Canon, a greater one than prayer otherwise had in the sacrifice of the ancients; the relationship between sacrifice and prayer in Christianity is given deep and telling expression. Both elements are intimately joined, so much so that the elements themselves have kept the name of the prayer of thanks said over them, and are called 'the eucharist'. The objective act of Christ and the concomitant act of the congregation sharing in his experience, his thanks, his praise and his sacrifice form together the Christian eucharist, the prayer of sacrifice, the high-point of Christian worship.

All about this climax, in smaller and greater circles group the other prayers, like smaller peaks on the slopes of the highest one. First of all come the prayers of the mass with the chants, and in some measure the lessons as well. Then there is the whole day office of the church, which we are to treat in this Chapter, the gold setting for the jewel of the sacrifice. Its first business, of course, is to give countenance and place to this sacrifice; but it is also lovely and valuable of itself. Another example from art will make the relationship even clearer. There are paintings which present simple landscape and atmosphere with such an intensity that some tiny figures are required to give the moving eyes a place of rest, or perhaps they serve simply to give the painting a name and make it more amenable to the public. In other pictures the action depicted so dominates the whole that the background seems to have no weight at all. Still other works have figures and background completely in harmony; the surrounding puts the figure into a proper frame, while the figures give the whole composition greater value: the line which starts up in the actors continues, so to speak, in the trees, buildings, and other natural features, and comes to rest in them; they for their part find completion in the main persons of the picture. Undoubtedly this last is a good solution of the artistic problem, and the church has constructed mass and office on this plan. The vast and monumental ideas which are hidden and silent in the sacrificial action, and which the canon seeks to express, continue in the office and are, so to speak, resolved into the spectral colours. Much that could only be hinted at in the centre shows itself in various places, and is submitted to loving contemplation. The course of salvation's advance in the old alliance, the preparations for the appearance of the Saviour, the incarnate Christ, his teaching, suffering, death and resurrection, his mystical continuance in the church, the sufferings and glory of the martyrs and other saints, the march forward of the saving work in church and individual—in brief, the mysteries of God's saving design and grace—are all depicted lovingly and presented in daily prayers, and these again find their crown and finish in the sacramental mystery of the altar; all the rich, varied lines converge upon the sacrifice and broken colours go back to a splendid shining unity.

So the office moves, as it were, about a firm pole, the presence and display in ritual of the great event which is the heart of the Christian thing: redemption through incarnation, death and resurrection. The prayer of the office shares in the sacramental value of the act of sacrifice, and is raised to the latter's objective worth. All the church's prayer and all the prayer of each man becomes the prayer of Christ. Christ's Spirit, the Holy Spirit, carries up the congregation's prayer on strong wings and gives it a divine worth which it would never have of itself. It becomes a real prayer 'in the name of Jesus', to which the Lord himself has promised sure fulfilment.[1] 'The man who abides in me as I do in him shall bear much fruit; without me you can do nothing. . . . If you remain in me and my words in you, you can ask what you will: it shall be done for you.'[2]

This truth, that the church's prayer is not, however exalted, merely the prayer of an isolated soul, but prayer with Christ, as intimate as the bride's conversation with the bridegroom, as the body's connection with its head, must be taken as a firm principle, if we would really understand the character and meaning of the office. The church prays; but in her the Spirit prays with unspeakable groaning.[3] The church makes petition, thinks and grows in consciousness, from the Spirit of Christ; it creates not merely human thoughts and feelings, or rather it brings them forth purified in the blood of Christ, glorified with the splendour of Christ. Of this prayer, too, St Paul's saying holds good: 'I live, no, no longer I, but Christ lives in me.'[4] All her words carry the mark of Christ her saviour, and are fashioned after him; all have passed through the atmosphere of his Spirit, and have a divine odour about them. All, therefore, have a meaning and a breadth which ranges high beyond every human meaning.

Upon this teaching rests a method of both practice and selection in liturgical prayer which is of very great importance, that of spiritual interpretation. The method is well-known; our Lord employed it, after his resurrection, after his exaltation to *Kyrios* and *Pneuma*. He 'interpreted the sense of scripture concerning himself'.[5] It was expanded by the apostles and fathers of the church. But it has a perhaps even more important place in the liturgy; of course biblical and liturgical allegory are often in harmony, as to method and object; their great principle is the same. But the liturgy, by selection and placing, and giving a point of view to the texts, gives new and special material to the allegory: it lends it new bloom, freshness and variety.

[1]Jn. 16, 23.   [2]Jn. 15, 5 and 7.   [3]Rom. 8, 26.
[4]Gal. 2, 20.   [5]Lk. 24, 27.

Allegory (ἀλληγορία) comes from the verb ἀλληγορεῖν (ἄλλος and ἀγορεύειν). It means to say something other than what is directly expressed; a second meaning is there beside the plain sense of the words, and must be attended to. Allegory in religion rests on the view that the divinely inspired author, or the inspirer himself, spoke in this hidden way, partly in consideration for human weakness and lack of development, partly because of the impossibility of expressing the things of God in human language; in this way more is shown to deep vision than a superficial view would indicate. The spiritual sense towers above the literal one; its high places are not open to everybody. Only gradually does the light of later events and revelations bring this sense into view; but when this happens, the words gain a royal splendour, and point to the peaks where God's thoughts are. The Old Testament in particular was the object of this allegorical interpretation. The fathers, with the light of faith to guide them, saw everywhere—in the law, the prophets, the acts of Old Testament kings and saints here more clearly, there less— the figure of Jesus, glowing in the half-darkness, until it emerges in the gospel's brightness. What the ancients gradually and wearily came to was as clear as noon-day when the world's own light shone: the keys to all mysteries were in Christ; when this unfailing instrument, the key of David, is put to the explaining of scripture, the whole beauty, depth and clarity of Christian allegory is seen for what it really is in the liturgy. Its heart is the redeeming work of Christ and everything we read and pray in these texts points to that. All of them open their deepest secrets; all become a hymn to Christ which the church sings. As the bride speaks of her lover, sometimes openly, sometimes in hidden approaches to meaning, the church sings, and the soul with her, of the bridegroom from heaven; at one time she uses the clear words of dogmatic formulae, at another mysterious images and poetry, the speech of love, which show only their depth and beauty to the initiate. The fate of mankind, the sacred history of the Old Testament as it is delivered in the lessons, gain its full meaning because the Son of God, mediator between God and man, appears as its centre, high point and end; in him the world and time find fulfilment. So Christ reveals himself in the liturgy as the Lord of all time, ruler of the earth, 'King of kings, Lord of lords',[1] as the leader of the people of God to everlasting salvation: he is God-man; only God-man could do all this.

Christ and the church: this is the content of the liturgy throughout,

[1] Apoc. 19, 16.

and so the content of the church's office—Christ, the God-man, the Saviour who showed himself to be the end and purpose with the words, 'I am the way, the truth and the life'.[1] The church, not the casual sum of Christians now alive, but the sacred communion of all who go to the Father through Christ, all who bear within themselves the Holy Spirit, and whom grace makes perfect like our Father in heaven: one sacred body, unified and enlivened by the breath of life, the *pneuma*; one supernatural dwelling house of stones, chosen for variety and beauty, and joined together, the stones dependent one upon another, make up a work of art. This church is not only content, but subject of the liturgy: it is the church which prays in the office.

This gives us the deepest ground for the 'givenness', the objectivity of liturgy we have so often spoken of before. When the bride, filled with the Holy Spirit, prays with Christ, her head and bridegroom, this is no prayer of individuals casually come together, but a prayer in the spirit of God and therefore in the spirit of truth received; it is the prayer in which the communion of all Christ's members join. That all of this aids the deepest and most personal conscious life rather than hindering it, is obvious; we shall come back to the consideration of this fact.

Considered in this way, the church not only stretches far beyond all national boundaries of one age, but from the beginning of the world to the end, from penitent Adam the just man, to the last saint at the world's end. All pray and work in the building of our liturgy. There are times when it grows in a lively fashion, springs up, when life in the Spirit of Christ and the body is so strong that it creates a forceful artistic expression for itself; the first centuries particularly were an age of this kind. There are other ages which have been less fresh, less rich; they keep the truth and goodness they have inherited, cultivate and hand them on. In no case is it 'historicism' on the church's part when she holds fast to the ancient and traditional fashion of her worship; rather, this love of what she has received comes from her very nature, from the timeless personality which we have seen, belongs to her; in a fashion she shares God's everlastingness. The church does not belong to yesterday; she need not be always producing novelties; she has treasures which never grow old. Therefore she is happy with tradition. Men, creatures of a single day, can come and go, with no joy in antiquity; the church can wait. Other generations will come to be grateful for her conservatism.

[1]Jn. 14, 6.

When, therefore, the church of our time makes her celebration one of rigid pattern this follows from her loyalty to tradition and a love for real value which rests upon her everlastingness. The deepest realism, however, rests not on a mere adherence to traditional forms, but in the mind of Christ and the church, which reaches beyond all individuals. The discipline of the church, of course, prefers to hold fast to the rites and texts which were created in Christian antiquity, and does so in the belief that those ancient times created what they did with a peculiarly high awareness of the church's mind. Realism and a sense of form here protect not merely inner reality: exterior discipline serves inward order and proceeds from it.

It is characteristic of the church that every individual group, a part of the body, and under the one head forms in its own time and place the image of the whole church; the whole church is in that place, by virtue of the small group's presence. St Cyprian writes in his *de Unitate Ecclesiae*, 'the office of bishop is one; individuals have such a share in it that each possesses the whole'.[1] There are, then, many bishops in the catholic church, yet their office has the mark of unity; their number brings no diversity into the church. So it is too, with the whole community. Where one congregation is united to its bishop, there is the church; there the church acts. Hence the ancients spoke of the 'church which is at Corinth', or just, 'the church at Corinth'.

We said earlier that the liturgy is the church's prayer: in practice this means a given community celebrating its office under the leadership of the priesthood. The community as such is therefore the subject of the liturgy; it enters this service as a community under discipline. Everyone takes his part in his own place: the bishop has one task, the priests another, the deacons another still, also the other clerics, virgins, and lay people. All together form a whole which praises God with one mouth.

From this it follows self-evidently that the office is to be celebrated in common, and, as far as the leaders of the congregation are concerned, in public. It will naturally be oral, then, audible and solemn as well.[2] A common silence like the silent worship of the Quakers is no liturgy, although Catholic worship too has periods of pause and silence.

Thus Catholic worship has strongly objective lines: they are

---

[1] *De Unitate Ecclesiae*, 4.
[2] It follows as equally obvious that the Christian must share personally in the community's worship, if he is not kept away for important reasons. Participation by artificial means such as radio is not enough.

expressed in its form. Nothing subjective or abitrary, no personal enthusiasm, momentary ecstasy or expressionism are to mark it; what it seeks are clarity beyond the limits of any single person, roots for a content that is divine and everlasting, a sober peaceful and measured expression of what belongs to it, in forms which give direction to the over-flow of thought and emotion, which put nature and passion within bonds. In this the liturgy shows herself the heiress of the ancient world for which the highest law of life and art was σοφρόσυνη, the observance of bounds; it revered order and measure as a reflection of the divine number and idea. Not lawlessness, lack of bounds, but things formed and measured, whatever their greatness and their depth, was divinity for the Greeks. The Book of Wisdom teaches that God has 'ordered all things according to measure, number and weight'.[1] Not chaos but cosmos is the work of the creating spirit. All the struggling powers are brought to their end and their harmony in him. The liturgy, too, knows how to moderate and bring to order the terrible struggles which, for example, run through the psalms.

The musical setting of the office is to be judged according to the same standard; it proceeds from the very heart of worship. The filling of men with the Holy Spirit, 'enthusiasm', must needs show itself in a song of the Spirit, as St Paul taught us; 'be filled with the Spirit, speak to one another in the Spirit's psalms, hymns and canticles, sing and chant the psalms in your hearts to the Lord'.[2] If every kind of music rises on the one hand from deep emotion, away from the triviality of daily life and mere calculating reason in the open spaces of the mind, on the other hand it possesses a deep vision of harmony and beauty in rhythm and number. The plenitude of God's power and the up-raising of the mind bring us into his freedom and order and lead to music, and music in pure, classical form. 'A lover sings,' says St Augustine.[3] The church says of love of God, 'he has set my love in order'.[4] So, too, her song is put in order: it is made an image of God's rest and of rest in God. No peace of the grave but movement, lasting flow, movement with purpose and rhythm, and, for this reason, restful. The music of the Latin Church, called Gregorian after Pope St Gregory who arranged it, is full of such peaceful movement and lively order. While there is often trouble and storm in the words, the music prepares the rainbow of peace, points to the harmony with no end. Sometimes the psalm melodies—usually

---

[1]Wis. 11, 20 (Vulg. 21).   [2]Eph. 5, 18 f.
[3]Sermo 256 *de Tempore*.   [4]Cant. 2, 4 (Vulgate).

those for the office—spread a sort of epic restfulness over the lyrical excitement of what the texts give us to sing. More mobile, yet with a steady measure, are the antiphons and hymns. Their task is to express the mood and words proper to each of the church's feasts, but they know better than to allow those moods a tone of excess or unrestraint. Fullness within limits, lively action in measure are the marks of liturgical form.

Language belongs to the very essence of liturgy. It is not the speech of every day, not the formal language of a single people, but a ritual language which age, tradition and history have made venerable: in the Western Church, Latin. A special characteristic of the language is that it transcends the national boundaries of the modern age, and gives recognition to a culture and religion which are universal. It takes us back into the Middle Ages, where the life of the nations was certainly vigorous, yet there was a real oneness in European culture as well, above and beyond their boundaries. The one Latin language gave the church in the West opportunity to display an *Imperium Romanum,* and in fact the use of the church's language depended on the continuance of the Roman Empire. In the Orient, where the Romans came up against a surface of hellenistic culture, the church keeps up Greek, Syriac and Coptic. But in these places, too, it is not a living language but an older, changeless form used specially in worship. This worship which turns to God, honours him and aims to lead men from all nations to him, prefers to use precise forms exalted above the language of every day, and thereby redolent of mystery, casting shadows of God's life. The mystery cannot stand in the crude light of day; it must show its supernatural worth in rare and precious vessels.[1] *Cotidiana vilescunt:* 'the things of every day grow base', is an old and true saying. At the same time, the foreignness of the language makes for greater peace in the liturgy. What might have a harsh and importunate effect in one's own language becomes more moderate, takes quieter and nobler shape in the splendour cast by ancient and holy words. So, then, liturgical language also performs a task which belongs to worship: it speaks to man of God, not in order to delude him about his pain and suffering, but to enable him interiorly, to overcome them and give him a taste of the glory of heaven, its happiness and harmony, as the sun at evening gives heat to the places of men's

[1] It should be noted in passing that our language, decomposed by subjectivism, is not, in any case, capable of expressing the divine, given, values of the liturgy, without purification and a raising of tone, just as our ordinary gestures cannot be taken into worship.

daily trouble and pain, brings them colour, clarity, and splendour.

The content of the office gives voice to the whole relationship between the Church and her members on the one hand and God on the other through the mediation of Christ; better, its content is the mystery of Christ and the church. We shall say something on this very broad subject later on.

Externally the office is made up in great part of texts from the Old and New Testaments. It is obvious that in her prayer the church should use the books which God himself has given her at the hands of inspired men. No one can speak better of all that passes between God and the church or her individual member than the Spirit of God and the man filled with God. Fundamentally the church did not simply acquire the sacred writings but bore them under the breath and guidance of the Spirit. Throughout thousands of years she has set down her experiences in them. It is no wonder that she is glad to fall back upon them in her worship; the inspired writings in the strict sense, those of which it can be said in a special sense that they are written by the Spirit of God and the church, end with the apostles. But the Spirit has not left his church; again and again he moves her to write songs of love and of wisdom; men and women sing and pray. What they have said has been both the deepest expression of their own hearts and at the same time something coming from the mind of Christ and the Christian community: it thus became everyone's possession; and as such it was taken into the cult of the church. Hymns, antiphons, lessons from the Fathers and teachers came into the liturgy along with the scripture: the bishops and other leaders of worship created, from their contemplation, the solemn prayers and prefaces: even the use of Scripture became an act of re-creation to the whole; music gave the final completion and consecration, bubbling up 'as the Holy Spirit dug in the hearts of holy men'.[1] Human things and godly things are joined in unbreakable conjunction.

This bond between God and man, between grace and nature, is, throughout, the essential mark of the Christian life of prayer. Until now we have emphasised its givenness, because the whole age of modernity, resting as it does upon man's self-rule and self-created experience has need above all to learn submission to the given, divine norm. The individualist consciousness of modern man 'emancipates' the personality and isolates it: in so doing it reduces society to atoms and clears the

---

[1] *Spiritu Sancto rimante in cordibus corum. Instituta Patrum* cited in Graduale Solesmes (1910) p. xiv.

way to collectivism; it sacrifices the person to the mass. The objective consciousness of community which the church possesses, submits the individual to a higher, God-given norm and gives it definite place; thereby it protects the personality, develops it and assures its status: place which belongs to it alone. The modern kind of order is a casual stone heap whose parts have no relationship to one another; they are pushed about, increased or diminished at will, and the picture they yield is one of immense confusion. The Christian thing is like an ancient temple which can be only as it is; in it every stone, every pillar, every beam and every statue has its place and displays its own beauty; together all the parts form a single work of art from which no part may be removed without injury to the whole. In this way liturgical prayer unites strong norms and respect for law with free movement and meaning for individual life. Even within the liturgy there are degrees of freedom. Just as ancient art, particularly Egyptian, Greek and ancient Christian painting and sculpture used the strictest forms for the greatest and most divine things, and then accepted freer movement as they came to human ones, yet avoided naturalism throughout, the church's prayer gives recognition to more volatile human feeling outside her solemn liturgical acts, and knows well how to express them.

It is neither possible nor necessary to depict all this in detail; some brief notes will suffice. We shall make them on the psalms, which are the heart of the office. In them no sort of religious experience is lacking; from deepest misery and sorrow, to abandonment and the full joy of oneness with God, from the feeling of oneness with the Lord's great congregation to the most intimate and personal experience of God; from the knowledge of God's dread majesty to enjoyment of his love: adoration, praise, thanks, the child's asking are all present. If, in addition, we take the allegorical interpretation regarding Christ and his church, the saving work of the new covenant, the changing lights which the festival, season or day have cast upon the psalm give us some shadowy glimpse of the inexhaustible riches of liturgical prayer. Usually the church tells us what use she is making of a psalm on a particular day and the mood she wants to express through it, by employing a particular antiphon as background or accompaniment. There are many of these refrains, or repeated verses; originally they were put in by the people after each verse or each three; now they frame the psalm, and come from it; their effect is, therefore, to make emphatic a particular theme of the psalm. Later, longer and more elaborate antiphons were created, to stand in looser connexion with the psalm, and lend it definite colour on a given day. The choral music, too, which is sung to the psalm, changes according to the musical tone of antiphon. One can see how simple and yet great are the means which the church uses here; the alleluia, for example, brings an Easter note to all the psalms it accompanies, even the serious *miserere*, and to the whole office an exalted and joyful aura.

Like the songs which David and the other God-inspired singers sang on their harps, the whole Scripture of the Old and New Testament, containing as it does an immense and inexhaustible sea of teaching, prayer, poetry and wisdom for living, is tuned into liturgy, and receives back from it a new and extraordinarily diverse life. Everyone knows how the prophecies, songs and sayings, the epistles and gospels are read, and begin to live, sparkle and send out new life. In addition the creators of the old liturgy who lived completely absorbed in the scriptures: men like Justin martyr, Origen, St Ambrose, Gregory the Great and many others. They applied these texts to the sacred mysteries of Christ and the church, and brought out gold to mint from the scriptures' rich mines. They did not proceed with the exactitude of a modern philologist, but with an artist's freedom, as ancient man loved to do; yet they did not become fantastic. Their vision went to the great things, to the whole picture. For this reason they opened up the mysteries of those inspired books. Their work is not a scientific reference work, but a free composition on God's word. Here is revealed how God's truth can become man's real possession. Cassian requires of monks,[1] that they should pray them as if they had written them. Christ is the first model of this; he prayed the words of a psalm, as he cried out to his Father in the depths of agony on the cross; so, too, the liturgy knows how to choose the right word from scripture for the right time, and to bring light from the other hemisphere into all the by-ways of this life of ours.

To inspired sources, then, are added the church's own creations, those of her saints, artists, teachers. The whole is a wonderful treasure. Different ages, peoples and ways of living, men and women, learned men, contemplatives have done their share in fashioning the garment which the liturgy has assumed to do God honour. How well the hymns, for example, give their own tone to each feast and season, so that a few words from one of them will call up before the mind's eye thoughts of the whole of it. How majestic is the Hymn for Christmas: 'Christ,

[1]Cassian, *Collat.* X, 11, 4–6.

redeemer of the world, the Father's only Son; thou wast born in ways beyond all speaking, before time ever was. . . .' Or the Hymn for Vespers of Easter, fragrant and intimate, binding together the mystery of Easter and the Eucharist, the true sacrament of Easter first food of the baptised: 'prepared for the banquet of the Lamb, clothed in white, the Red Sea past, we will sing to Christ, our Prince. His sacred body, his rose-coloured blood, his body, made ready on the Cross we taste, and live for God. We are protected from the angel of vengeance in the paschal night, set free from the hard yoke of Pharaoh. Our pasch is Christ now; he was sacrificed, as a lamb; as pure bread with no leaven his flesh was sacrificed.' A mixture of joy, love and longing marks the Hymn for Vespers of Ascension: 'Jesus, our salvation, love, our longing, God the creator, man at end of ages—how could goodness stretch to bring thee to bear our sins, suffer a terrible death, to set us free from all death. . . . Be thou our joy, as thou shalt one day be our prize. . . .' And on Pentecost the song is of the Spirit who moves the winds, full of power, like the rush of a great bird's wings yet gentle as a dove's song: 'Come, Creator Spirit, come: visit the minds which are thy own; fill with godly grace the hearts of thy own making. Thou art called the advocate, gift of the most high, living spring, tongue of fire, fire of love, oil of anointing. Thou art seven-fold in thy gifts finger of God's right hand, his promise, giver of tongues to speak. Light the flame within our spirits, pour thy love into our hearts, stiffen weak bodies with staying strength of thine. . . .'

Let us look briefly at the variety of lessons from the writings of the Fathers which form so pleasant an alternation to liturgical prayer. Each Father mirrors the light of Christianity in his own fashion; the writings of each differ in point of view, mood, content and form. There is sober exegesis, and then suddenly a burst of allegory; there is theological depth and practical wisdom, then mystical fires rise. But always it is a voice of deepest culture, and the most profound grasp of Christianity; often there is high and classical form as well.

Responding to measured variety of content are the vast and lively differences in carrying out the office, the result of which is that it is never monotonous, never tiring, but keeps the mind always fresh. The psalms rise and fall at a gentle pace; the melody is simple and pleasant, and for all its liveliness and constant exchange between the two choirs, spreads an epic peace over the whole. On the other hand the melodies are not lacking in lively variety. Each of the eight tones in which the antiphons are composed and according to which the psalms are sung has its own character: by its choice of tone, the church gives each new song its own proper colouring. The second, for example, is full of longing, the fourth more mystical, the seventh festive; the fifth full of deep emotion, the eighth strong and masculine. Still more precisely fitted to this varying content are the antiphons, which with their short, clear lines of direction, their freshness and buoyancy are miniature works of art, moments of Greek movement beside the oriental stillness of the psalms. When the mind is weary of the psalms' prayer and the burden of soul-searching they contain, the versicle brings up a shout at the end, like a blast of trumpets, breaking the monotone of the peaceful line, and passing on to something new: reading, petition, or the high points of the office, the Magnificat or Benedictus. These last in turn are sung in a specially solemn psalm tone, the eighth, for example, which recalls a royal march. The lessons have a simple tone of their own, which takes away all personal rhetoric, but leaves clear the divisions of meaning. Responsories follow the lessons; they are marked by a rich, solemn, slow-moving melody, and by the repetition of parts, as one choir answers the other. Thus they give shape to the moment of after-thought and contemplativeness which revolves deep, slow thoughts, and considers them now on one side, now on another, returning with alacrity to old sayings that can never be wrung out. The so-called long responses *responsoria prolixa* usually come in matins which have a particularly contemplative character, and join the lessons, with their stimuli to new thoughts. The short responses are usually found in Lauds and Vespers; one such may show how deep is the grasp which these forms of prayer have for the working of men's minds and prayer, and how finely they express the simple things they have to say:

℣   From the lion's mouth, Lord, deliver me
℞   From the lion's mouth, Lord, deliver me
℣   Lord, deliver me
℞   From the lion's mouth
℣   Lord, deliver me

We can see and hear in the text and melody how this prayerful cry first springs up and forms itself in the soul of an individual or a few devoted persons, and then passes over to the whole community; a second, stronger cry is added; the choir stays with its first petition; the whole comes to rest in slow stages, and ends in a repetition of the first phrase by all which at the same time means that it has been heard. The hymns run more quickly in the same direction; their charm and liveliness is Greek. The church was very long in taking them into the office; only the activity of St Ambrose brought them gradually closer to the church's seriousness. Then their light, impressionable, characteristic tone began to set the mood for the different feasts, and to give a stronger feeling to the individual days; as creations of the West they represented action as against the Oriental psalms, even more than the antiphons, of which we have already spoken.

In the last section we spoke frequently of the psychological basis for liturgical prayer and told how it became stylized in liturgical form. The structure of the office, too, both of individual hours and the day as a whole, is a psychological masterpiece. We shall give a view of the whole day office at the end of the chapter; here we want only to remark how some of the hours develop, Terce for example. After a moment for recollection, a cry of petition goes up to God, by which the leader also, so to speak, rouses the group: 'O God come to my assistance'; then the community answer, 'O Lord make speed to save me'. The *Gloria Patri* and alleluia which follow bring rest into this stormy cry, and at the same time mark the aim of the hour and its joyful character; then comes the freshness of the hymn, expressing briefly and clearly its meaning. At least one antiphon is struck up, to bring in the themes of the day or feast. The three psalms follow which make up the heart and high point of the hours: the antiphon is said. All of this brings the soul into the deep world of contemplation. But it cannot stay there forever; it grows tired, needs new stimuli; these come from the short lesson. From contemplation the soul passes at the versicle to petition, and so up to the intentions of the church, man, and the day: Lord have mercy; Our Father, then the special prayer of the day. With the verse of praise, *Benedicamus Domino* the brief, rich office closes; here was contemplation of divine truth, praise, thanks, adoration, petition: all drawn into one, every kind of prayer in its proper place.

The psychology of Vespers is even more striking. More psalms, given character and thrown up into a particular light by their antiphons, make up the contemplative element. Here too the weary mind is refreshed by a short reading from the scriptures, and then, in the Responsory, returns to the contemplative prayer we have mentioned before. The meditative response is followed by the melodic hymn, strongly connected with the day, its effect a fresh and lively one. After a versicle to lead the way, comes a particularly well-constructed antiphon for the Magnificat, which usually summarises clearly a feast's themes, and then carries its effect through the praise hymn of the Holy Virgin, enhancing its beauty. The Magnificat itself sinks deep into contemplation of the deep things of God and makes the offering of a humble mind to God's infinite love: it is the high point of the feast. When we go beyond it, it is to the *Our Father* and the prayer of the day; the latter, of course, is wholly caught up in the great mystical mood of the Magnificat. The structure of the morning and night services which belong closely together, is also quite remarkable. Three times we sing, 'O Lord open thou my lips,' 'and my heart shall declare thy praise'; dulled minds are called out to the joy of God's life. The prayerful psalm three puts the hindrances to prayer out of the way, so to speak. Then begins the invitatory, the great invitation, through which an antiphon runs, like an encouraging promise of all the feast's thinking, in the shortest possible space. In Psalm 94 the happy encouragement to be glad in God's presence stands side by side with earnest warnings, even threats, to the careless and the hard of heart. When the hymn is over, the mind is sufficiently awake and prepared. Now we come to the real purpose of night worship, contemplation. Vast, mysterious, difficult psalms pass before the soul's eye; the mysteries of God make themselves known in hard phrases. The soul wrestles with God for salvation, for knowledge of him. It joins its voice to the words Christ speaks in the psalm; it lives the life and suffering of the Lord with it; with him it hates sin and turns to the divine light; sees the miracle of God's mystical city, goes out in longing beyond the confusion and darkness of the world into God's freedom and clarity; it longs to go over out of the confusion and darkness of this world into God's freedom and clarity; it mourns loneliness and abandonment in this world, the faithlessness of men and is happy with the one true friend, God. Still, who could exhaust in words all the depths of contemplative prayer in the psalms? When the soul is weary of this pilgrimage on the high places, it goes down to the fresh waters of scripture; in the responsories it carries on its contemplation. Again a series of psalms and a refreshing group of lessons there follows. In the third nocturn come the shorter, brighter Cantica, songs from the prophets or wisdom writings; a homily from the Fathers goes with the gospel, interrupted and slowed down by responsories preparing for the appearance of Christ in whom all the difficulties of inner life find their solution. Yet before Christ himself appears in the gospel, the confident hope of the church breaks out in the majestic, powerful hymn *Te Deum*, which praises the Trinity and the Saviour, and at the end passes over to humble petition. Now the light of the world himself appears, and spreads his light over all the difficulties and confusion of church. Man's longing is fulfilled, the high-point of the office is here: the Lord speaks. So with a short word of praise and the prayer, Matins ends, and the mind gives itself to that jubilation which already sounded in the *Te Deum*: it grows stronger as Lauds progresses and reaches its far highest point in the *Benedictus*, the wonderful song of praise for the redemption in Christ. Throughout the whole of this as of every office, the church shows herself mistress of the deepest psychology, the psychology of prayer.

Before considering the psychological and artistic strength of the Day office, we should refer to a very important matter: the relationship of liturgy to nature. The polytheism of the heathen made the powers of nature divine, and submitted man to them; this 'service to the elements' often has great sensible joy, but ends in evil and in terror of the terrible power of nature which takes a man up and, after brief sport, destroys him. Pantheism makes man feel his oneness with the whole web of the cosmos; but this daemonic feeling, too, leads to the enslavement of the spiritual in man, to the tyranny of sense, and to panic before the predatory beasts which lurk in unredeemed nature. More or less pantheistic, restless and full of muddy emotion, and 'sentimental', is the feeling which the Romantics had for nature. The gnostic overestimates the evil of nature, treats her like something evil, is full of fear before her, runs from her; he is 'full of the sorrow for things'. The Christian too, knows that nature groans under sin, along with man; it longs for redemption, which will come to it when it comes to the children of God. But he also knows that nature is a work of God's; because it is, he can love it, see in it the print of God's passing. Yet he stands over it; nature is tool and image of the spiritual. The liturgy, therefore, from the very beginning, from the time when the Lord made bread and wine the elements of the mass, has given nature its part to play. The church was not afraid to take over natural symbols which the heathen had used in their worship and, by putting them into proper place, to give them their true value. By doing so she has made them holy, just as through the sacraments and sacred gestures, she made the human body; in fact the church has given to nature the first fruits of glory, the gifts of the children of God. For our theme the symbolism of light is of particular importance, connected as it is in the first place with the sun. This phenomenon in nature is much more striking to a Mediterranean than to us, because in that region its forms are so vivid and definite. The sun really stands in the heaven like a dread king, spreading terror and blessings: *sol invictus*[1] as the ancients called him, the author of the 18th psalm among them. Terrible majesty glows, burns from heaven; it wakes life and kills it, giving life and blinding the eye that is too keen. It is no surprise that first orientals and then dwellers of the Mediterranean region should have honoured the sun-king as their high God. Even the philosophers gave it honour: Plato regarded the sun as a symbol of the good which was the sun in the kingdom of spirits. But in later neo-Platonism and the heathen religions of the first Christian centuries the invincible sun god was the centre of worship; this was expressed in many prayers. The morning light above all was revered as something divine. In Northern Europe and America one is fonder of broken colours, light and dark patches, where fantasy and emotion can be lost in muddy clouds. The typical man of antiquity had a sense for clarity and truth, for the genuine and the whole; he valued above all the dawn light with its unlimited fullness, 'glorious as on the first of days, as it streamed out of the hand of God over land lying dark and still a little while before; it streams up and gives things back their colour and brightness; it awakens life and joy. The East, therefore, a symbol of God, became itself divine; men turned to it when they sought God in prayer. Evening like morning was especially a time for prayer; yet the other phases of the sun's course all had their meaning in worship too.

The church has nurtured these ideas insofar as they are true, but purified them of their limitations, of their enslavement to the elements. For her the visible sun is not the godhead; it is, as Plato has already glimpsed, a symbol of the Spirit-son, Jesus Christ the incarnate Logos, who in the life of nature as in the world beyond wakens life and spreads it, as he himself says, 'I am the light of the world'.[2] So the church has set up her office according to its changing course, and thereby given it new depth and beauty. 'Grace builds upon nature': it is fitting that man should fashion his daily life of prayer on the great image of nature, and give back its beauty, spiritualized, to the creator.

Still another point for brief consideration is the warning of Christ and the Apostles, 'pray always'. How does the church fulfil this command? In mind she is always with the Lord, as the Lord is always with her.

---

[1]The unconquered sun god, particularly Mithras.   [2]Jn. 8, 12.

This cannot be carried out literally, in external worship, but she none-theless fulfils it. For in accordance with the ancient view there is a kind of earthly eternity in like, regular recurrence in time. As time renews itself in the regular movement of the years and moons, and by this continual re-birth becomes in a sense eternal, so an event becomes celebrated 'eternally' by being celebrated every month or year. The *sollemnitas*,[1] yearly feast, becomes *aeternitas*, everlastingness. The cele-bration of the church year, especially the sundays, rest on this principle. Always the mysteries of salvation are carried out in the same rhythm; they become eternally real, until the solemnity in heaven passes into eternal reality in every sense of the word. The exhortation to pray always has been carried out by the church's praying each day at the same ap-pointed times. These hours (*horae*), are laid down according to the sun's course; as we have said, the sun is a symbol of Christ. Historical occurrences from the life of Jesus yield symbolic meaning, or fall in with such meanings. Thus the sun's rising is the most striking image of the Saviour rising from the dead, and in fact the hour of his rising; Sext, the time he was nailed to the cross, but according to ancient tradi-tion the hour of his ascensions as well, the high noon of his life; None was the hour at which he died on the cross. At the third hour of day, Terce recalls the out-pouring of the Holy Spirit.

Thus prepared we can consider the course and construction of the daily office. It begins on the previous evening, with 'first vespers'. For the ancients the day did not begin at midnight, a point which can only be determined by mechanical means or a mechanical clock; it ended when the sun went down, and the new one began. The service of wor-ship held at the hour of dusk in the evening light (vesperus, ἑσπέρα, evening) belongs in time to the day before, but leads over to the day following. Hence at least the second part, and on great feasts the whole vespers, belongs liturgically to the feast of the following day. The mind is led into the ante-chamber of the feast's circle of ideas, and receives a first taste of its content. This is especially well expressed in the first vespers of Christmas.

As soon as the sun has disappeared behind the horizon, a new day begins in the night. Out of the night day rises; this deep consideration of ancient man which only children seem to have kept until now (they often reckon in nights) is the measure for the liturgy. The construction of the day office has its firm foundation in the night service.

[1]From Oscan word *sollus* (like Latin *omnis*), and *annus*: 'event in every year'.

The night gives darkness and silence; in it we see far out into the stars, feel comfort and dread, know the smallness of man and the greatness of his spirit: night is the time of great yet single vision. For Christians it has lost the terrors which pursued unredeemed mankind, but kept its sweetness, recollection and gentle dread. So it became the proper time for prayer, for raising the mind up to God. The work of ordinary day is over, consciousness less disturbed by the outside world, the ear enjoys valued stillness, and the stars give light. A shadow of eternity rests on the night; time seems brought to a point. For this reason the Romans called the night *intempesta*, timeless. The heathen had already shown preference for night in their deeper and more moving rites; the mysteries in which they hoped to be conjoined to God were celebrated at night, with no light but flickering torches, until the moment came when the light of the mysteries flamed up and told that the God was at hand. The church also celebrates her greatest mysteries, the incarnation, the resurrection, as they occurred, in the dead of night. The greater feasts are begun with night watches, vigils. Like the Greeks with their παννυχίς, the ancient church watched the whole night through before a principal feast, with prayer, song and reading. Holiest of all was the night of Easter, in which the splendour and glory of the risen Christ came streaming out of the passion's deep darkness, and brought the sunrise in high heaven to man who sat in the shadow of death. In the night these Christians of the early church waited for Christ to return: 'this is the night which shall be celebrated with watches for the coming (adventus, παρουσία) of our God and King. Its essence is twofold; after his suffering he returned in it to life, and later he will enjoy in it the Lordship of the wide world.'[1] There is a note of mystical expectation lying on all vigils:[2]

> This is the very time
> when, as the gospel tells,
> the bridegroom shall come one day
> the Lord of everlasting heavens.
> The holy virgins run to him,
> run out as he will come
> They bear their lamps along
> and have their fill of joy.[3]

[1]Lactantius *Div. Instit. VII*, 19. Cf other passages in Franz *Die kirch. Benedictionen im Mittelater* I, 1909 p. 519 f.; Tertullian, *De Baptismo* 19.
[2]A. Löhr: 'Der eschatologische Gedanke in den Ferialhymnen': *Lit. Ztschrift*. 4. p. 11–21.*
[3]From the hymn for midnight, *Mediae noctis tempus est* (fifth century).

Monks kept such a vigil every night, and because it was not possible always to watch through the whole night they took certain hours of it. This night celebration (called Matins, because held in the early morning) is all devoted to contemplation. The mind moves contemplatively, praying, loving the infinite thoughts of God; it struggles with the spirit of God, as Jacob once fought with the angel until dawn, and finally won God's blessing and the name Israel—who wrestles with God. Thus strengthened the soul can enter into the great mystic actions of the holy mass, carry them out with understanding and worth.

The night is over, the light comes in the first brightness of morning: the stars grow faint; only the pale morning star shines on. The church begins her morning service of praise: *Laudes*. The soul comes out of its deeper contemplation, and passes on to acts of praise and thanks. It can never be content with its praise; it must call up all creatures to help it in this work. Christ is already near, the sun of justice, the church's healing. The dawn of morning which precedes him is rosy: the Ambrosian hymn speaks of it: 'dawn goes up her path; let the Son, true dawn come all in the Father, as the Father is in him'. The mind looks in longing to that 'last morning' when it will see the divine light which will never be extinguished. Then at last, the sun comes like the victorious hero Christ after his long night of pain, blazing from the tomb to blind the watchers. This is the moment for the schola to begin the hymn of praise to redemption in Christ:

> Blessed be the Lord, the God of Israel
> He has visited his people
> and wrought their redemption . . .
> Salvation from our enemies, and
> from the hand of those that hate us . . .
> passing all our days in holiness,
> and approved in his sight . . .
> Such is the merciful kindness
> which has bidden him come to
> us, like a dawning from on high,
> to give light to those who live
> in darkness, in the shadow of
> death, and to guide our feet
> in the way of peace.

The sun goes higher; light calls to work, to the burden and heat of the day. It is the first hour, Prime. Before going out to work the Christian puts on the armour of prayer—plain, simple prayer, full of thoughts for the weariness, the earnestness of work, of petitions for help against difficulties which can come from both evil spirits and men. All the 'little hours' carry this strong character of petition, particularly Prime; the depth and exuberance of the night and dawn service has not gone out, but come to rest in the heart. Now is the time for work. The sun has lost the bright freshness of early morning and gone up into the heaven.

We think about this ripening power of God's living warmth, at the third hour, Terce, as we celebrate the descent of the divine *pneuma*, the *calor verbi* and sing of it in our hymn: Holy Ghost, one with the Father and the Son. Pour thyself out into our hearts and fill them. Mouth, tongue, unconscious and conscious mind, all life's powers are to sing praise of God, let its love spring up in full fire, its glow light the neighbour.' But the psalms tell of the misery of exile, of longing for the home country, of looking out to the eternal mountains of salvation and the Lord's city, Jerusalem.

Sext is prayed at the heat of mid-day when the mid-day demon goes about to bring harm to body and soul; it begs for cooling to the heats that do harm, soothing of contrary strife, health and harmony of soul and body. All that is what it hopes for from the Lord, to whom alone it looks, as the servant to his master.

The ninth hour, None, brings relief to the heat. Rest is at hand. The petition is for a bright evening, a holy death, and eternal glory after a life of weariness. The soul sees itself already free from imprisonment happy to gather the sheaves and bind them and enjoy rest with those it loves now rest is done.

Now the sun goes west, and descends. The marvellous play of colour at evening, the glory which spreads itself over the tired earth gives men a certain sight of the other, better kingdom; evening is ready to bring sorrowful longing for peace, harmony and unity to the heart of man. The ancients thought that the kingdom of the dead and the islands of the blessed are found in the West, where the sun goes into the sea. The Christian, too, is glad to think at evening of a happy departure from this world's weariness, to the light that stays. When St Ignatius of Antioch takes up the word sunset in his epistle to the Romans, he thinks immediately of another setting, and writes, 'It is good to go down from this world and rise in God'. In this mood the church sings second vespers; after the psalms, responsories and hymns in which she has buried herself in the feast, she intones the *Magnificat*, the high song of the virgin of virgins which, so different from the strong, masculine freshness of the *Benedictus*, is deep, tender, as it were feminine. In it man thanks the Lord for the overflow of happiness he has experienced, for all the Lord, ever true to his promises, has done for him. Union with God, the great aim of all prayer and all worship finds its clearest expression in the *Magnificat* at the end of the day office. All the joy of liturgical prayer leads to oneness with God, and flows out of him again: 'And my spirit rejoiced in God my Saviour.'

Compline ends the day as a quiet night prayer with no special meaning.

If now we look back once more on the many questions with which the church's office confronted us, and the answers we gave, brief and hesitant though they were, it remains clear that the liturgy is as broad and as deep as the life of Christ and His church, the life they have in the Father. The liturgy is a hymn of love; at one time the bride praises the bridegroom, and then the order is reversed; at others it is they two who praise the Father. God's truth plays in the liturgy like sunlight in water; for liturgy is founded upon the words of Scripture and the fathers, upon an infallible, dogmatic faith. But it is in itself a stream flowing from God's great goodness; it does not merely teach, it leads to love. In it the word becomes a song of love; and where truth and goodness stand together beauty will not be lacking. In the liturgy God's truth is given form and shape, and so becomes a work of art, not through isolated aestheticism or dilettantism but of its own weight.

No other prayer can challenge with the liturgy's right, to hold God's truth, God's goodness, and God's beauty, and to send forth their splendours; no other is so near to the heart of Christ and of his whole church. In the last centuries has not the office become too much a mere duty while more intimate piety has passed over to the so-called devotions? It is our business to give back to the office its proper place, to make it once more what it is and has a right to be for us. God's honour and men's salvation cannot be separated: both proceed from the one great sacrifice. So too the office brings both glory to God and healing to men. 'The sacrifice of praise does me honour; it is the way on which I shall reveal salvation' (Ps 49).

EDITOR'S NOTES

p. 4. Generalizations about the history of spirituality always involve a certain risk. They are, so to speak, long range shots, and do not have the same measure of validity for every individual phenomenon. What is said in depreciation here and on the following page is meant in the first instance only for those schools, above all the Christian ones, which gradually estranged themselves from the church. It cannot, then, be applied without any modification to legitimate developments within the theology and piety of the Church, after the Renaissance. But at the same time we may not overlook the great complexity of give and take in such movements; hence, it is possible for the criticism expressed here, if a sharp one, to have its justification, even of matters within the church.

p. 13. The great theme of Casel's presentation is the oneness and uniqueness of the sacrifice of the New Testament. The Lord sacrificed once; he does not sacrifice again. But in her sacramental ritual action the church is so taken into the one sacrifice of Christ that in every new action of hers that one sacrifice of his is present. This corresponds wholly and entirely to the teaching of the church as expressed in the encyclical *Mediator Dei* of Pope Pius XII, even though there is, nonetheless, room for disagreement about the kind and manner of this presence. Pius XII wrote: 'in order that individual sinners may be washed in the blood of the lamb, the cooperation of the Christian faithful is required. For although Christ, speaking in general, has reconciled mankind, the whole human race, to the Father by his bloody death, he willed that they should come, should be drawn, by the sacraments and the eucharistic sacrifice, to his cross, in order to obtain the fruits of redemption won by him through it. As we have already explained, Jesus Christ dying on the cross, endowed his church with an immeasurable treasure of redemption, to which she contributed nothing at all; but where it is a question of the distribution of this treasure, he not only gives his chaste bride a share in the work of sanctifying human beings, but wills that this work should, in a manner, arise from her action. The august sacrifice of the altar is as it were a most precious instrument by which the merits of the redeeming cross are distributed to those who believe: "as often as the commemoration of this victim is celebrated, the work of our redemption is fulfilled" (Secret of the 9th Sunday after Pentecost). Far from this detracting from the value of the bloody sacrifice of the cross, it underlines and makes clearer its necessity and greatness, as the Council of Trent emphasizes. For as it is offered daily, it reminds us that there is no other salvation except in the cross of our Lord Jesus Christ, and that God wills the continuation of his sacrifice . . .', (second 99.) (Encyclical Mediator Dei ASS 1947 p. 551 seq.)

p. 15. St Paul's teaching on baptism has been in the forefront of interest in the last few years. Cf the brief bibliography in the editor's preface to this volume, particularly note seven. Here we would recall only the paper by Victor Warnach, '*Die Tauflehre des Römerbriefs in der neueren theologischen Diskussion*' (A.L.W. V/2, 1958, pp. 274–332).

p. 15. The words of Cyril and their use are disputed. Casel translates and discusses the passage in A.L.W. I (1950), 140–142. He says in the course of this exposition, 'Cyril here contrasts the (natural or historical) reality with the sacramental imitation of the saving act; the one is the model, the other the image. By the presentation of the image, the believer takes a share in the original; through the one he reaches the reality of the other, yet without again posing its natural reality, which is, of course, unique . . .' (140). See the next comment on p. 39.

p. 16. To determine more precisely the degree of reality which this medial thing has is the thorny task of theology in our day. The first fully scientific labour, under Casel's stimulus, as it were an inaugural study, was G. Söhngen's *Symbol und Wirklichkeit im Kultmysterium* (1937). It was followed by Victor Warnach's article in *Liturgisches Leben* 5 (1938): '*Zum Problem der Mysteriengenwart*', and Casel's own articles in J.L.W., particularly 15 (1941), 253–269. The latter works are critical of Söhngen. In the last-named article Casel formulated his point of view in these words: 'In the knowledge born of faith we see in the sacramental image its original, the saving work of Christ. We see it in faith and *gnosis*, that is to say, we touch it, make it our own, are conformed to it through participation and re-formed after the likeness of the crucified and risen Christ . . . Sacrament and original saving act are not two separated things, but one; the image is so filled with the reality of the original deed that it may rightly be called a presence of it' (op. cit. p. 268). A valuable contribution to the explanation of the mode of this presence has been made recently by J. Betz and his proposal of 'commemorative actual presence' (cf the work by him cited in note 9 of the preface). P. Polycarp Wegenaer in his book *Heilsgegenwart* has emphasized the Thomist concept of the *contactus virtutis divinae*; the contact of original saving act and sacramental activity, whereby the power of God is conveyed.

p. 17. The expression which we may find harsh, 'the Lord became Spirit *pneuma*)' is formed in a way consonant with the usage of Scripture: Cf 1 Cor. 15, 45 and Jn. 7, 39. The adequately correct formulation in our language would be, 'the Lord, raised up, became Spirit, that is to say, was exalted to God in his humanity as well, having his throne at God's right hand . . .' Cf Neunheuser 'Der Hlg Geist in der Liturgie': *Liturgie und Mönchtum* 20 (1957) 11–33, esp 29 ff.

p. 17. This must of course be understood to mean that baptism itself, even without subsequent confirmation is a beginning of communication of the Holy Sprit. Cf Neunheuser, *Taufe und Firmung* in the new Herder *Handbuch der Dogmenschichte* IV/2, p. 39 ff, esp p. 40 and 57.

p. 18. The unusual implication as it may seem to us once again corresponds to the usage of scriptural language: the passage cited before, 2 Cor. 3, 17 ὁ δὲ κύριος τὸ πνεῦμά ἐστιν. Casel himself gives an interpretation a few lines below of the equivalence: Christian = other Christ = Spirit which is wholly in keeping with the usage of present-day dogmatic theology.

p. 21. The teaching on sacrifice here and in the pages which follow corresponds wholly and entirely to the requirements of the Council of Trent in the XXIInd session (Denzinger 937a ff) and the encyclical *Mediator Dei*. To the extent, however, that they pass beyond those requirements (it is well-known that these pronouncements of authority did not seek to solve the questions in controversy among theologians) their particular aim, in Casel's mind, was the presentation of the numerical unity of Christ's act (Cf. J.L.W. 6 (1927), 193, where he speaks of the identity of the act of sacrifice in mass and cross); in the historical act of Christ's sacrifice in its temporal moment and in the act which the church is always performing, there is but one single sacrificial act of Christ. Because the church presents this sacrifice by her action, she makes the sacrifice of Christ; she shares in it through her sacramental service, and beyond that she is bound to join herself to the one offering which is present by her own wholly personal activity.

p. 30. The Old Testament of course knew no mysteries if we understand the term in the full sense of the NT; it is in this sense that the following lines use the word. But this does not prevent us from speaking in concert with e.g. Hebrews, 10, 1 and the majority of the fathers about mysteries or sacraments in an imperfect sense. Thus St Thomas answers the question whether there had to be sacraments after the fall yet before Christ (III, 63, 1), in other words, under the Old Testament: 'The first sacraments to be celebrated and observed by the law were heralds of Christ to come, and it was necessary that the coming of Christ should be announced; hence it was necessary that there should have been sacraments to prepare the way for this coming of his. . . . These sacraments were certain sensible signs of invisible things by which man is made holy . . . signs by which man gave testimony of his faith in the coming of the redeemer; such signs were called sacraments.'

p. 31. Earthly salvation and earthly goods: long life, daily bread, the continuance of the people in its land flowing with milk and honey, etc. These must however be seen very much as a symbol of things beyond this level; as their promise and foundation. They were in fact a means for the Israelite who faithfully performed his duties towards God of obtaining everlasting salvation.

p. 32. Of course the world of the Old Testament failed when faced with the greatness of the revelation of God's merciful love in the New Testament. But it failed less because this revelation was of a different spirit from its own than because God's revelation had *not yet reached such final possibilities*. Not even the forms of the Indo-germanic peoples reached this highest stage of divine revelation. This does not mean that some elements of their achievement were not to have a special meaning, thanks to God's providence, in a later time; that is surely what Casel means. There is still much to be done concerning the details of this matter; we may mention Padberg's article (Note 14 of the preface above) and one by Victor Warnach: A.L.W. V/2 (1958), p. 331 ff.

p. 34. It is most important to keep this in mind. The all-important fact is that Christianity is a mystery religion in virtue of its own very nature and the liturgy of mysteries is the central and essential activity of this religion. Cf above p. 52. The question of the concrete manner in which the mystery terminology was brought into the church, particularly the development from hellenistic *mysterion* to Latin *mysterium* and *sacramentum* in profane and Christian use is a matter of special interest and not a closed question. Of interest is A. Kolping's review of Fittkau's book on the mystery in Chrysostom: *Theolog. Revue* 51 (1955), 24–28.

p. 35. It is certainly correct that in the heart of the Christian Middle Ages with its new Northern peoples and their formative influence upon that age, a new climate of thought arose, one at first tempestuous and excessive, as in Abelard for example. But it was very largely taken in hand by the great figures of the golden age of the universities, and placed at the service of a new and different but nonetheless truly Christian synthesis. The evil consequences which Casel names here and on the following pages are phenomena of a markedly later age, in which the synthesis had come apart. To the extent that the attitudes of modern anthropocentric thought remain within the church's circle of influence they can constitute a real value, even in these forms of piety; where the church is, there is the mystery as well. Casel's judgment on this development is perhaps too negative.

p. 37. The proper thing here would be to list all the work done in the last decade; I content myself with recalling Filthaut's book and the other notes on more recent work in the A.L.W. Cf supra, notes 1–7, page x, and 1–2, page xi. Not least is it important to realize that there is a difference in Casel's great work between elements which are simply exegesis of the plain if somewhat structured teaching of faith, and those which are his own conclusions, a further development of the traditional data. Casel sought only to work in the first way; but he may well have underestimated his own work in the second genre.

p. 38. It is well to compare Casel's definition with that of liturgy given in the encyclical *Mediator Dei*: 'Sacra igitur liturgia cultum publicum constituit, quem Redemptor noster, Ecclesiae Caput, caelesti Patri habet; quemque christifidelium societas Conditori suo et per ipsum aeterno Patri tribuit; utque omnia breviter perstringamus, integrum constituit publicum cultum mystici Iesu Christi Corporis, Capitis nempe membrorumque eius.' (ASS 1947, p. 528–9).

p. 51. The fact of a change in the form of piety cannot be denied; but in judging it we must in any case remember that its beginning in modern times even if centred on the self, anthropocentric, must by no means therefore stand opposed to a truly liturgical and church-oriented piety. Pope Pius XII says in *Mediator Dei* 'If the private and personal piety of the individual neglects holy mass and the sacraments, withdraws from the saving influence which flows from head to the members it will without doubt become a reprehensible and fruitless thing'. But this does not need to be. When modern forms of piety are rightly integrated in the spirit of the church, in proper and organic relationship, made 'theocentric', to use the word of the encyclical, they can be of great value for the liturgical service itself.

p. 52. In order to evaluate properly what is being said here, we must remember that the 'communal mysticism of antiquity' which is praised can be preferred to the mysticism of modern times only in the form in which Christianity gave it. The dark adumbrations of hellenistic cults could in no way be preferred to modern Christian mysticism. Casel's picture here is of ideal types.

p. 55. Casel has advanced on what he says here in the article which was published in A.L.W. I/1 on the mystery language of St Paul. A good introduction to the whole problem is to be found in the book of Victor Warnach: *Agape*, Patmos 1951 (a translation is to be published by Darton, Longman & Todd). Chapter: *Die Agape als Mysterium*. The question of mysterion is treated (German), on pages 372–374, and the extent of the mystery presence, (German) on pages 389–91. A good survey of the latest state of the question of St Paul and the mystery religions of his environment is to be found in Warnach's article 'Die Tauflehre des Römerbriefes', A.L.W. V/2 (1958) p. 329 note 117. Among other things, Bornkamm's article in Kittel's *Wörterbuch* should also be mentioned: IV (1940), 809–834. None of these questions have found final answers; but the fruitfulness in discussion of Casel's original stimulus should not be overlooked. It has made possible a truly Christian explanation of the healing Christ has brought, realized in the church and its sacramental, liturgical actions; it has made possible as well a reasonable explanation of the wide use of the words *mysterium* and *mysteria*, *sacramentum* and *sacramenta* in the language of the classical Rome liturgy. Through it too is made possible an historical picture which holds pre- and non-Christian cults in their proper relationship to the salvation which God has accomplished, salvation which is not without its witnesses outside the realm of revelation.

p. 60. Cf the note on page (37) and the literature mentioned there.

p. 63. One might mention the additional material in 'Beiträge zur Theologie des Kirchenjahres' in *Liturgie und Mönchtum* 1950, No. 5 and 'L'Année liturgique selon Dom Casel' in *Questions liturgiques et paroissiales* 1957, p. 286–298.

p. 90. A book by Dom Casel's disciple Aemiliana Löhr has further developed these thoughts in an admirable way: *Abend und Morgen*, Pustet, 1955.

INDEX

ALSO IN THE SERIES

Romano Guardini
The Spirit of the Liturgy
Introduction by Joanne M. Pierce

A profound reflection on the nature of liturgical worship

0-8245-1777-6 $12.95

Henri de Lubac
The Mystery of the Supernatural
Introduction by David L. Schindler

A seminal work presenting the core of Henri de Lubac's theological vision.

0-8245-1699-0 $ 27.50 paperback

At your bookstore, or to order directly from the publisher, please send check or money order (including $3.00 for the first book plus $1.00 for each additional book) to:

The Crossroad Publishing Company
370 Lexington Avenue, New York, NY 10017

We hope you enjoyed *The Mystery of Christian Worship* Thank you for reading it.

herder &
herder